A good

for a book

RAGGA & THE JACK MAGIC ORCHESTRA CD front [1997]

EYE OF THE STORM

THE ALBUM GRAPHICS OF

STORM THORGERSON

WITH

PETER CURZON

AND JON CROSSLAND

SANCTUARY PUBLISHING

TEXT:

Storm Thorgerson

BOOK DESIGN:

Peter Curzon and Storm Thorgerson

PRINTED IN:

Hong Kong

PUBLISHED BY:

Sanctuary Publishing Limited,
45-53 Sinclair Road, London, W14 ONS,
United Kingdom

COPYRIGHT:

Storm Thorgerson, 1999

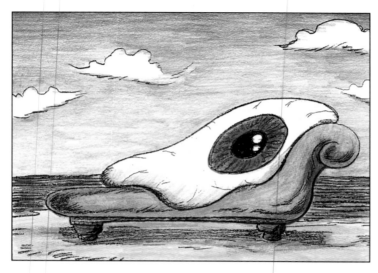

EYE OF THE STORM
THE ALBUM GRAPHICS OF STORM THORGERSON

Many thanks to:

John McGill for artistic contribution.
Clare Howells and Kirsten Shaw for typing.
Keith Breeden, Paul Maxon and Andy Earl for visual input.
David Gale for some editing.
Carl Lyttle for studio space and bonhomie.
Nick Stone and Kate Klinger for invaluable assistance
in the production of this book.
Douglas Adams, David Gilmour, Ian Dury and Rob Dickinson.

Eleanor, Mark, Sarah, Helen, Tony and Roger at
Pip Printing, Belsize Park.
Paul, Darrin, Reed, Steve, Jayne and all at Sonicon.
Rob and John at Classic.
Suren, Andy and Mark at Unichrome.
John and all at FTP.
Robin at Tapestry and Richard Baker at Metro.

Rob O'Connor, Mark Kaylor, Ian Wright, Colin Chambers,
Alton Omer, Adrian Smith, John Lewis, John Robertson,
Julien Mills, Jeremy Clarke, Chloe Mason and Hannah Evans.
Aubrey Powell and Peter Christopherson.
Penny, Merck, Jeff, Eddy and Michelle at Sanctuary.

Dedicated to my son Bill who has made my life sonnier.

Foreword

Storm Thorgerson is the best album designer in the world. I say this partly because he's a friend – one of those wild eyed, staring kind of friends that you really want to stay on the right side of – but also because it's patently true. Look at the evidence. By which I mean look at your collection of LPs.

Now, I'm not one of these vinyl snobs. I'm very happy with CDs, in all respects other than one. All right, two, if you include the fact that the cases are made of some special super-breakable plastic which is guaranteed to shatter if you drop them from six inches onto a soft bed. But the thing I really miss is that vinyl LPs used to be twelve inch square works of art. *With The Beatles*, *Sgt Pepper*, *Dark Side Of The Moon*, *Wish You Were Here*, *The White Album*, *Animals*, *Exile On Main Street*, *Atom Heart Mother*. Anything strike you about the list? The majority of them are Pink Floyd albums, all of which were designed or co-designed by the same person, Storm Thorgerson. (Storm used to work with Aubrey 'Po' Powell in the brilliant but extremely badly spelled Hipgnosis design team.) He is a perfectionist in his pursuit of the completely absurd. Nobody else in the world (at least, nobody currently at liberty in the community) would go to such Herculean efforts to line up dozens and dozens of identical and immaculately made up beds on a beach for no reason at all. It's dumbfounding. You know that this was not a momentary lapse of reason. It must have been at least a month of meticulously deranged behaviour.

CDs are a problem, though, for artists like Storm. They are just not big enough. They are quite big enough, thank you very much, for pictures of George Michael sniffing his own armpit (what on earth was he thinking?), but they just don't offer the scope that LPs used to. Storm brilliantly overcame this limitation on *The Division Bell* by making the CD cover just one little instance of a hugely multi-faceted piece of imagery which spread with endless variations over every piece of design connected with the album and the world tour. The myriad parts all hinted at a much, much bigger whole, which must exist because otherwise why would anybody go to such monumental trouble to adumbrate* it?

Of course, Storm has always done a ton of other work besides Floyd albums, which these days come around less often than governments. There have been covers for albums by Led Zeppelin, Peter Gabriel, 10cc and more recently, Catherine Wheel, The Cranberries, Ian Dury and other fine clients; book designs (including one slim volume entitled *The Hitchhiker's Guide To The Galaxy*); as well as actual Art. This book you are currently holding gives you some idea of the depth and breadth of his extreme inability to see the world the way that normal folks do.

Though it's clear from looking at his pictures that Storm is some kind of mad genius, the really interesting thing, for those who know him, is that his pictures are the least weird thing about him.

Douglas Adams

* 'Adumbrate': I put this word in here because I think that more people should take the trouble to look it up.

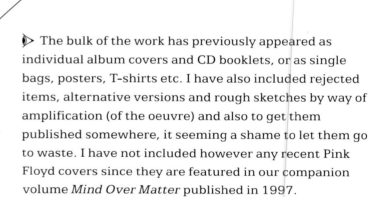

Pre FACE

Before you are exposed to the real thing, before you sample the wares so to speak, a little word in your ear. The majority of the images and designs in this book have been produced in collaboration with colleagues; they are the fruit of several minds, formed by loose and changing liaisons, especially with graphic designers Peter Curzon and Jon Crossland, photographers Tony May and Rupert Truman, and storyboard artist Finlay Cowan. To these I extend my deep appreciation and affirm my enduring respect. ◁ They are not, however, responsible nor would they want to be, for the views and opinions which are the sole responsibility (and psychosis) of your humble author. Nor are they responsible for any errors, omissions or critical comments. Whilst every care has been taken I apologise for those still overlooked, except of course where clearly intended. ◁

▷ The bulk of the work has previously appeared as individual album covers and CD booklets, or as single bags, posters, T-shirts etc. I have also included rejected items, alternative versions and rough sketches by way of amplification (of the oeuvre) and also to get them published somewhere, it seeming a shame to let them go to waste. I have not included however any recent Pink Floyd covers since they are featured in our companion volume *Mind Over Matter* published in 1997.

▷ Life may be tough but titles are a nightmare. The script for *Shakespeare In Love* contains a wonderful running gag about the difficulty (and importance) of getting a good title, and good names for leading characters. *Romeo And Juliet* was originally and fetchingly called *Romeo And Ethel The Pirate's Daughter*. Similarly I was called 'Storm' but only on arrival, having been 'Geraldine', would you believe, for the previous nine months. Though the title of my book may be open to some improvement it was hard to resist in view of its appropriateness. (And *Eye Of The Geraldine* didn't have quite the same ring.)

▷ But one can't judge a book by its title, can one?

▷ Or a person by their shoes?

▷ Or reality by its appearance?

▷ Or an album by its cover?

Storm 'Geraldine' Thorgerson
March 1999

Contents

Introduction

It's what you do, not how you do it

by

Jean-Luc Cliché

NECK OF THE WOODS

In a tiny wet corner of the world called England, in the sprawling town of London, in the north of the city, in a small enclave called Belsize Park, in a little nondescript studio, amongst working folk of many different pursuits, in the profession called commercial art, and in the lesser field of graphic design, and in the still smaller area known as album graphics, in the even smaller category of photography, in the subdivision of creative photography, is where you'll find me and my colleagues.

▷ From this restricted microcosm it is difficult to provide the more usual kind of introduction to a book of visual imagery. I cannot easily give the context, for example, because I'm in it, up to my neck, and I am not a historian, though I wish I were (see p40). I cannot offer much in the way of a critical overview because I am too emotional to be detached, and I am not a critic, though not without critical views of course. It is hard to assess the cultural and/or artistic importance of the work that follows not only because it is unbecoming for the artist himself to do so, but also because one is dogged by the suspicion that perhaps there isn't any. And I cannot reveal personal psychological life and its relation to output being rather shy and unsure of its relevance anyway, and not being a biographer nor a gossip, except at parties.

▷ It seems to me that knowing the private lives of artists poses an interesting problem in terms of how it affects one's response to their art. My beloved and I recently visited a Vermeer exhibition, and shortly after a Picasso portrait retrospective (we are so cultured, my dears!), and came up squarely against this dilemma. Hearing about Vermeer's private life shed interesting light – and that's the key word for Vermeer – on his compositional preoccupations, on the economy of subject matter (half his paintings consist of a woman near a window), but also on his sustained exploration of the aforementioned light. Picasso, on the other hand, painted a large number of portraits of the many women in his life, and when these are viewed in conjunction with a pictorial history they put him in a very questionable position! The portraits were generally as unflattering (distorted, cubist and ugly) as his affairs were numerous. Maybe he was a brute, since his paintings are brutish. Despite a wonderful sense of line, form and shape, like perfect pitch, he had no interest in light, precious little in colour and rarely showed touching or affectionate tendencies. Perhaps Picasso didn't like the women in his life that much. The question is: does one gain insight when apprised of the (private) lives of artists, or is one better off viewing the work in (relative) ignorance? ◁ But I digress already. My private life may or may not have a bearing on the work I produce – well it obviously does in relation to its origins and its formation, but probably very little in terms of your appreciation – but my work environment certainly does. Unless you are unswervingly tenacious, single minded to a fault, or in the thrall of pharmaceutical substances, it is nigh on impossible to remain impervious to surroundings. In album graphics, both the artistic and (particularly) the business side can get to you, and although I try, of course, to remain calm and collected I sometimes become a little peeved, as you'll notice, and a number of critical, sarcastic, ill tempered and even childish comments might emerge. These outbursts, asides and comments are like post-it notes from a beleaguered studio, thoughts and reminders stuck on the wall, or above the telephone or on the edge of the VDU or near the fax, and are common, if not de rigueur, in many studios across the land. The following post-it notes are of course from my particular beleaguered studio and are in no particular order. ◁

CATHERINE WHEEL Sony promotion [1999]

So there I was, glancing through a large photography book published by Taschen, and thinking how photographers possess a selective eye and I have a conceptual eye. No judgement here, just description. Photographers select snippets of reality (by and large) that they come across (or revisit), and then endeavour to capture them in their own particular way. They select either a specific angle, or time of day, or find themselves at a certain spot, or arrange to do so. They select people, pets or trees to focus attention. And they augment this admirable faculty (which may be innate and/or taught) with a variety of personal and technological add-ons, like extra lighting or forced development, tonal printing or accentuated blacks. Cartier Bresson is deemed to have a selective eye par excellence, whereas my aunt, Elsie, God bless her socks, does not. Cartier Bresson is a photographer, and an artist, whilst Aunt Elsie is a snapper and not an artist (though she might have something to say about that).

▷ Designers like us have the conceptual eye. The photographs we take, for example, are not just arranged but are conceived from nothing. Ideas concretise as visions, or 'takes', and are intended to represent the music they accompany, or more precisely, the feelings and ideas embodied in the music. Our images are not selected from external reality, though they may comprise extremely real elements, but are 'selected' from the imagination, ie they are conceived. Nothing is captured, all is arranged. Props, models and locations are not discovered but are envisaged, and then requisitioned to suit. I am not much concerned with what exists – at least in my work – but with what is conjured in response to the feelings and ideas in the music. It is probably axiomatic that the images are not real, are not found pictures, and could not be found by others, but are clearly wrought by hand, by eye and brain, like the music. The designer's conceptual eye is besotted with artifice, not with spontaneity; not reality, but in the rearrangement of reality to fit expression, and to fulfil communication.

▷ I suspect that the selective eye exhibits a greater care for the details of the medium than the conceptual eye. I am not that bothered about photographic issues, though I should be. I am primarily interested in how well feelings and thoughts are represented, only secondly in whether it is professionally and photographically speaking a good photograph. Moreover photography entails an ongoing frustration because it is neutral, cold and reality based, whereas my intentions are to want the opposite, and to continually seek out the expressive, passionate and imaginative qualities. So I love photography and I hate it. Got to use it, but I'd rather be a painter (though I can't draw). In fashion photography the eye is largely selective but is also in small measure conceptual, devising

THE SELECTIVE/CONCEPTUAL EYE

We tend to use photographs in our work. Solutions to graphic problems, namely what to put on album covers, are usually photographic. But I am not a photographer. I have used Nikons, Hasselblads, Rolleis, Sinars etc. I have used B/W film, colour negative, colour transparency, infra red and high speed. I have photoprinted, dye transferred, reverse printed, solarised, computered and collaged. I have shot indoors, outdoors, behind doors (but not The Doors), in various studios, and on more locations than hairs on the chest, but I am not a photographer. Other photographers also would not, I suspect, call me a photographer; a jumped up designer maybe, but not a photographer. ◁

circumstances best suited to enhance the clothes. In still life as well, or in certain studio portraiture, where lighting and objects are 'imagined', and then arranged. The individual elements still exist in a separate reality, though, not like the ingredients in many of our designs, brought into existence solely for the image, and then erased afterwards.

REPRESENTATION (NOT COMMERCIALITY)

The main objective of our album designs is to represent the music of the album in question in visual terms. This may sound obvious but it is not, said the walrus, quite that straightforward. When advertising music product the powers that be (record company people, managers etc) do not wish to use the physical product (ie a CD, which is just a piece of plastic), nor usually the actual music, which is intangible (except in radio advertising), but rather the

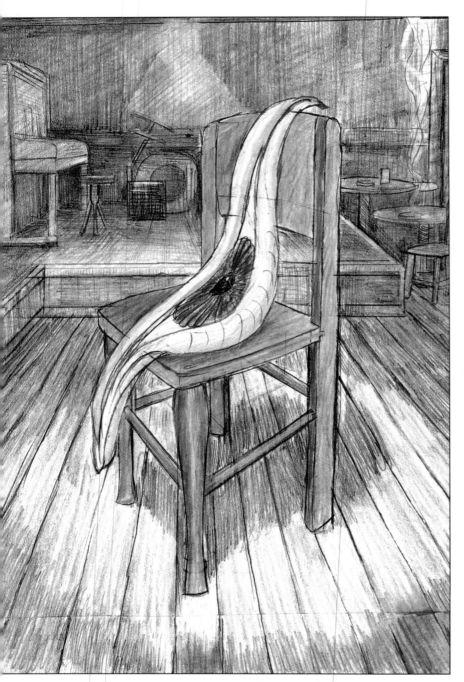

ideas in the music, the personalities of the musicians who create the music, or even the lifestyle that might be (mistakenly) associated with it. Record companies reasonably believe that the advertising, and hence the packaging, though these do not necessarily go hand in hand, should be geared to selling records, and this may not be the same as representation. The so called commercial or marketing outlook not only has drawbacks for general creativity, but has severe limitations for design variation (preoccupied with big type and brash imagery), for integrity (it doesn't care if it's true), and even for sales, the very reason for which it is invoked. This is because any connection between shifting product and the nature of design is unknown, unverifiable and unresearched. If record companies knew what graphics helped sell records then they would use them regularly, and would probably re-invent them time and time again. Such a connection between sales and graphic design is a chimera and probably

doesn't exist, unlike interior or fashion design where it is clearly pivotal. You can't judge a book (or an album) by its cover, now can you? Everyone knows that, except of course marketing men at record companies. ◁
The issue of representation for them does not necessarily figure strongly, but for us it is paramount. It is the guiding light, closely linked, hopefully, with creating good and effective design – design which evokes somehow, somewhere, a degree of feeling, or a set of thoughts, or some questioning, the odd smile or a sense of incongruity. In a word, good communicative work. Twin peaks – representation and effectiveness. Selling records is further down the list – quite a lot further, actually. ◁
Thus representation can afford to be quite obscure, innovative, tangential, controversial, bizarre and so on and can be rendered in any suitable medium. It might possess a delayed effect since it is not so impact

"SHARKS" vinyl front [1978]

orientated, perhaps creeping up on the purchaser when at home – a concept so alien to marketing precepts as to be blasphemous and hence ignored. (Pink Floyd's 1976 album, Wish You Were Here, had a design tailored for home enjoyment which was hidden from view in the shop by an opaque shrink wrap that had to be broken – an act only possible after purchase.) Representation allows the designer the freedom to be as expressive as the music or even more so, and not to be confined by the restraints of populist taste, crass commercial criteria, and the uncultured minds of record company market people who often don't know shit and who don't consult experts or initiate research and who, in the end, are as predictable as tabloids. Design, at least in my book, works best when inspired by the music and the passions and ideas embodied in the music, and when the designer does his level best to emulate or add visual meaning and visual gloss (not matt) to the recorded entity. ◁

Bones of contention are clearly discernible, then, between record company and designer. They can also exist between record company and recording artiste, especially when the latter feels that covers and music are so closely linked that they want a say in how it looks, in the same way that they have obviously a big say in how the music sounds. Bands get into arguments with the record company, even to the point of denying the need to sell, or at least relegating it to a desirable but not overriding criterion. Their case is strengthened by the fact that, as pointed out earlier, nobody knows the nature of the link between sales and design, if one exists at all. Pink Floyd managed to get to Number One and sell a few million copies of Atom Heart Mother, without a band photo, or any commercial ingredients. Nothing. Just a cow. Years later record company personnel still insist that lettering, big clear lettering, helps sell a record. Pink Floyd, they say, could sell in a paper bag. Precisely. The cover design is not necessarily or primarily there as a sales tool – after all, many best selling albums have lousy covers – but to stimulate and entertain instead, to provide a visual extension of the music within, and to present information attractively. ◁

And it does not matter to me what kind of music it is, or if one likes it or not. I do not demand of myself that I must like it in order to represent it, as some of my distant colleagues do, claiming that unless they like the music they can't think of anything. From the start I felt it was snobbish to assess one type of music over another, and narrow minded to implicate others in one's own preferences. I like and dislike many kinds of music; more particularly I dislike some practitioners of types of music I like in general. So I don't ask if I like the music in question, I just play it and see if I respond, see if hearing it makes me visualise something, which it usually does. And I often get to like the music I'm working on even if I didn't in the first place, partly because I listen to it so much, and partly because I want to believe in it, so I can believe in my imagery more easily. But not always, for that would be too good to be true. ◁

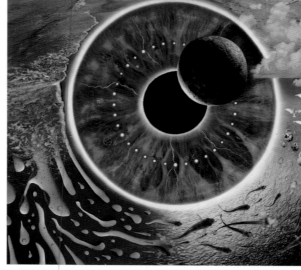

PINK FLOYD "Pulse" CD box [1995]

demanded by the design. Though the idea for the design is the first and crucial step, it is stillborn without adequate, if not superb, realisation. And that is when we do it for real. Whether it is building a large metal ball, or hanging people upside down from a great height. Or squashing naked youths into small wooden boxes. Or putting people on tall poles, or immersing hapless swimmers in icy rivers, or submerging dancers underwater for unreasonable periods. Or constructing an armchair the size of a generous house, or making a teddy bear robot, or a model hot air balloon. I don't fake it. I organise the making or finding of these 'real' or hyper-real ingredients, which I then re-locate to some extraordinary and particular spot to be photographed, and then rendered as a finished image. All the parts are real and physical, but not necessarily at the same time or in the same place, and not necessarily in the order one might think. The final amalgamation attempts to confound expectations of normal reality by essentially, and contradictorily, being composed of real parts.

▷ This conundrum is, I suspect, central. I hope to ring the changes on reality by using it against itself, not by escaping into colourful fantasy or baroque excess, or alternatively into pure graphics or any number of computer generated worlds, but by taking the reality building blocks and rearranging them. Sometimes quietly and without fuss, hardly noticeable by some (the tree on p115 is often viewed without seeing the head shaped topiary); at other times with full fanfare (the Anthrax

DOING IT FOR REAL

In terms of a technical ethic my basic inclination has been to do it for real. That means constructing or finding, arranging or positioning whatever actual ingredients are

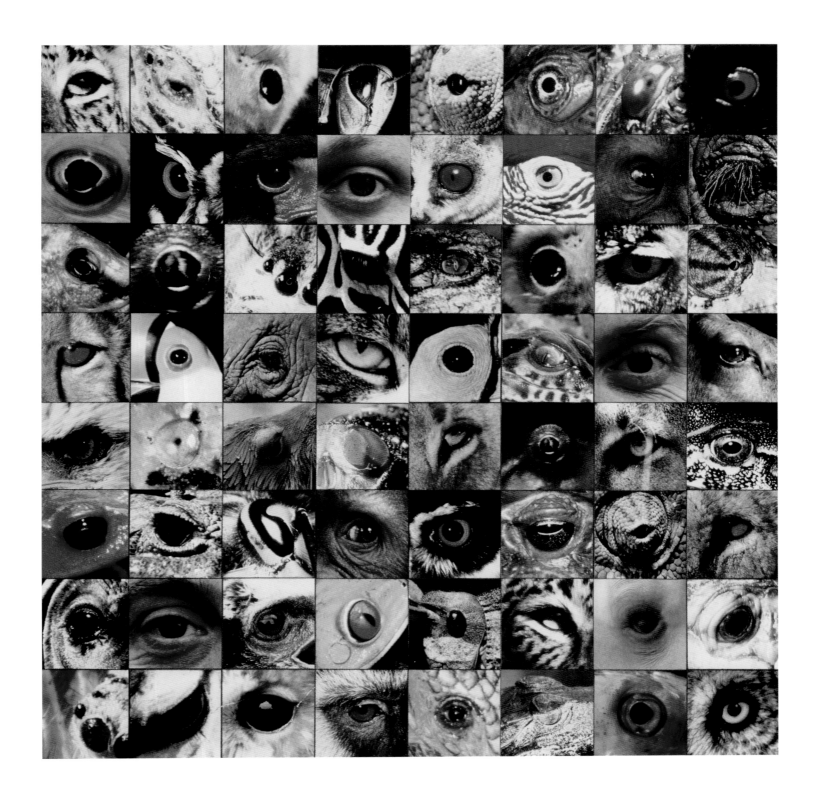

GENTLEMEN WITHOUT WEAPONS "Transmissions" vinyl back [1988]

information shorthand. People value their albums and become attached to the accompanying designs, sometimes as much as to the music, and on rare occasions consider them worthy in their own right. Well I would argue that, wouldn't I? Otherwise I might be hard put to warrant, or to have even bothered with, this book.

metal ball on p69). Ironically then I need photography – the premier reality medium – to fulfil my ambitions and to render my unreal, but real looking, images in the most effective manner. But I am not a photographer. As an image maker who likes to mess with reality, I'm inclined to use a medium which a large part of me finds cold and removed. A detached, inexpressive medium for, hopefully, passionate, expressive ideas. No wonder I'm confused! ◁

IMPORTANCE (OF ALBUM GRAPHICS)

My post-it notes from a beleaguered studio were going to avoid this issue as too difficult and involved for personal comment, but then I changed my mind. I don't want to short sell anybody. If I want the prospective public to value what I do (and the music I'm accompanying) I don't need to submit insubstantial stuff, or unreal items that pretend a reality. We do it for real because, by and large, it looks better, but also because we're honest merchants. (Sickening, isn't it?) No expense spared, no excuses given. If it's important to me, I want it to be important to you. Well, a bit. ◁

I think also that album covers are important since they are the only other items which last as long as the music – which can be quite a long time. The cover stays, when much else slips away, when record companies change, managers are fired and groups disintegrate or retire. Album graphics, like book covers but nicer, are permanent packaging, sitting on one's shelf or rack for years, viewed and reviewed often, especially when the music is played. Album covers may also be deemed important as a field for innovative photography and contemporary graphics. Or as a barometer of fashion and taste. Or simply as an

ENEMIES OF MEANING

"It ain't what you do, it's the way that you do it" intoned Bananarama many moons ago, extolling the virtues and merits of style over content. That old chestnut. It's the way it looks, my dear, not what it means. How something is presented is what matters, not its implications. This particular philosophy is endemic to popular music and is determined mostly, I think, by the transience of teenage hormones. I mean 'transience' only in a temporal sense. I don't mean that teenage hormones aren't important (to teenagers, long suffering parents and record company marketing departments), or that they disappear for good (though sometimes for us old toadies it certainly feels that they have). Rather that the adolescent rush, the excitement and newness, soon dissipate because one gets used to them. Teenagers are characterised by the surprise, by the not knowing what these hormonal changes are or how to accommodate them. But let's face it, after a few years they learn to live with and enjoy their hormones, and hopefully those of others. More to the point, behaviour becomes moderated by other factors such as acquiring one's own money; and fleeting enthusiasm eases off, transience lessens, and the purchasing of music products becomes a more considered affair. Taste becomes more defined and more enduring.

▷ Fashion and style are skin deep and ephemeral by nature. My view is that we need something that lasts. Meaning is what we need. Resonance, ideas and feelings. Something that can have wider and longer appeal. Even in the shallowest waters of popular music there lurks more complex feelings. The simple epithet 'get down and have a good time' is susceptible to representation and can thus contain meaning. But no, the music industry fosters an aversion to meaning as if it were some kind of contagion, and the battle cry 'it's how it looks' continues to hold sway. Because the music business is populated by insecure and unqualified people, this axiom is sustained longer and in far more instances than necessary, applied unthinkingly to bands who aren't suited, and to design items (album covers) that don't need it. And this aversion to meaning is further perpetrated by the music press where journalists chastise meaning by describing it as pretentious, over the top, heavy, significant and other rabid adjectives. Meaning won't bite, nor get in the way of expression (feelings), but the music industry and even some musicians don't believe this, swayed instead by fashion, or persuaded by marketing departments, in turn citing the retail trade as evidence, that meaning is bad for image, and hence for 'sales'.

▷ Meaning here means a variety of things including, but not restricted to, the expression of moods, exploration of feelings, posing of questions, floating of ideas, positing theories, displaying ambiguities, commenting on politics, criticising rationality and so on and so forth. Graphic design which is both consonant and resonant with the feelings and ideas in the music. Something to get the emotional and mental teeth into.

▷ This rambling argument in favour of meaning is not

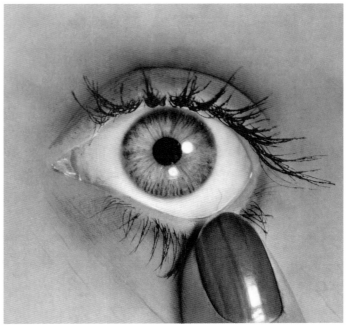

anti style nor against the way something looks, only against enemies of meaning. Of course the way design looks is vital, I know that. The look and the style need to be carefully researched and diligently applied otherwise the meaning that they are trying to express might be sabotaged. How lighting works, how models are dressed, props and sets designed, what colours and focus are deployed – all these are crucial in their own right, but more expressly, are essential for conveying the meaning. A strong feeling or stimulating idea will not be communicated well by inappropriate and ugly styling. It's simply a case of style servicing the meaning, not vice versa, a case of not allowing the style to subvert the idea…unless of course the idea is crap…or purely decorative.

▷ Mind you, I and other designers, being fussy and anal from birth, worry greatly how the smallest type or the most subdued of colours, or the smallest uninvited speck may look. But I didn't always, not in the early days when

I was as obsessed by meaning as much as those I'm criticising now are obsessed by style. Fellow designer Keith Breeden characterised the bulk of my work (pre 1984) as great ideas badly put together and poorly designed. Fucking cheek. So I persuaded him to work with me, not because he has a fine mind and is a great illustrator, but so he could clean up my act and make me and my work look better.

CLICHÉS AND NEAR CLICHÉS

Every graphic designer tries, I'm sure, to be innovative and to design new and exciting stuff. At the very least he or she tries hard to avoid the mundane and the obvious. Tries to avoid clichés, in other words. Visual clichés are the graphic designer's nemesis. They stifle creativity, suffocate the spirit and eventually put one out of business. I detest visual clichés like smiling suns, fluffy kittens and Valentine's hearts, so tired and overused they negate what they are trying to say. Clichés may be a cultural phenomenon but are keenly felt to be the antithesis of good design, and consequently to be avoided like the plague. ◁

But things are not so straightforward in real life (they seldom are, I hear you say) and some visual motifs sail close to the wind, looking very like clichés but not quite, being described perhaps as 'kitsch' or 'naive'. Some designers use clichés on purpose as a critique of the visual medium or of the cultural climate (so they claim), and some clichés are used as satire, or reworked in a new and challenging way, or represented so lovingly, like a Norman Rockwell, as to be a cliché of a cliché. Notwithstanding these exceptions, clichés are just clichés, tired old shit best left alone. ◁

And then to my horror I realised that despite my talking (of clichés) and whilst writing this very introduction (to the book), my work contained clichés. How embarrassing but there it is, or rather here they are: loads of cliché eyes. As soon as I realised, I felt it only appropriate, if not poetic justice, to include them here to show, if nothing else, how easy it is to come a cropper. Nothing like

mouthing off and having it come back in your face. I would like to think, fancifully, that these many eyes are evidence of a revealing and detailed exploration of an icon (eye con). In some instances (p13 and p134) I believe this to be true, but in others I have no defence.

▷ A more generous way to assess these numerous eyes is to describe them as recurring motifs which held fascination for the obsessive artist – that's me – and reveal inner workings and emotional preoccupations. Not to be too lofty but Van Gogh liked his sunflowers, Max Ernst his moons and Dali his beaches. Other motifs of mine are, I notice, water, nudes, beds, open landscapes and an assortment of animals. Also devices such as visual ambiguity and receding perspective. I like odd juxtapositions and contradictory scale, and there are often people or figures involved, not always defined, indicating a narrative or evoking, hopefully, some memory or emotion. I favour a central point of view, and I prefer formal cropping, but I shall refrain from further analysis and leave others more qualified to draw psychological inferences or make artistic connections, if indeed there are any.

▷ Extending the word 'cliché' to cover other tired and lame old graphic devices, design tricks and commercial attitudes, permits enumerating the following dislikes, in no particular order. I hate the marketing clichés of bold type, huge logos, prominent bar codes, impact driven images, corny sex and posey fashionable lifestyle type imagery. Also 'clichés' of vanity perpetrated in the form of numerous band photos: girl groups in soft porn poses, boys in baggy wear and midriffs, moody soul singers or aggressive looking rap artists and leather clad hard rock practitioners – all promoted by managers, record companies and musicians themselves who can't be bothered or dare not ring the changes. Nothing wrong with portraits, just with predictable ones. Clichés of graphics, like cool or geometric layout and computerised backgrounds, intricate lacy lines, or distorted and repeated typography (computers have a lot to answer for).

Clichés of plagiarism where commercial design gets passed off as innovative, and lauded as such, whereas in fact it is clearly stolen from previous sources, such as Rodzhenko and constructivism, reappearing in contemporary magazines and on record covers under another name. And where images are borrowed from libraries or old masters and redeployed as contemporary design with only the slightest alteration. And clichés of preciousness, when graphic artists get to believe in their own enveloping importance and get fiddly or terribly neat and mean with both their work and their information.

▷ Shopping one's friends no doubt? Biting the hand that feeds perhaps? Just angry post-it notes from a beleaguered studio somewhere in the ordinary suburbs of North London.

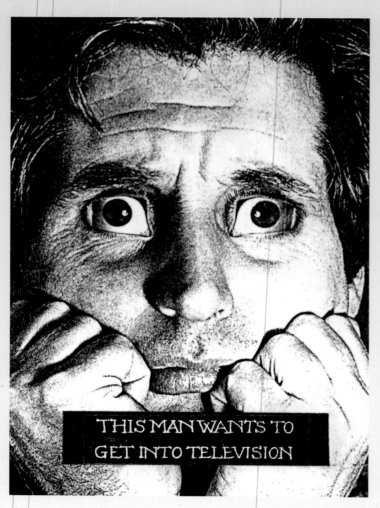

THIS MAN WANTS TO GET INTO TELEVISION

Storm Thorgerson

HALF APOLOGIES

I make little or no apology for the egocentricity of this book in so much as it is a given, whomsoever compiled it. Artists are egocentric by nature. Graphic artists are no different. I do however offer my half apologies on two other counts. Firstly and briefly for sounding off. Re-reading this introduction tends to appal, not so much for its content, as for its presumption – the nagging realisation that what I personally have to say is simply not that important. In mitigation I'd like to point out, provided it is not further calumny, that in order to write at all requires a temporary belief that what one has to say is important. I also reckoned that if you were kind enough to purchase a book about my work then you should get my waffle as well. You don't want someone else's waffle do you?

▷ Secondly I'd like to half apologise for my childishness, which you will find in parts of the text to come. This issue is quite complex, not, I think, just a case of owning up and offering apologies, even half apologies. In short I have decided, for my sins, not to delete all my childish outbursts. These include some sharp, but nasty, comments and some cheap cracks at the expense of targets who can't answer back right here, though they can somewhere else if they're so inclined. These outbursts, though tinged with a degree of virulence and sarcasm, betoken genuinely held beliefs, valid criticisms and warranted anger, but appear in print, if not in life, as childish things, reeking of petulance and tantrum. Me childish? Can't be, I'm an adult. And risky as it is, presumably adult enough to expose my childishness. I can't offer you much of an overview, or context, or self critique but I can offer you some exposure to the psyche, as artists are traditionally supposed to do. Just what you always wanted, right? – more squishy psyche. In the meantime, dear reader, welcome to my exposure, photographically speaking.

(Sundry) Portraits

The camera never lies

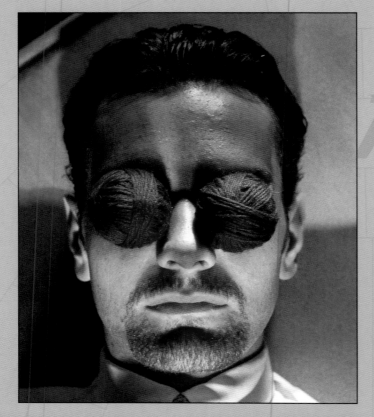

My good and talented friend Jill Furmanovsky is an excellent portrait photographer, amongst other things, and takes pictures of politicians, authors and musicians. She tries to capture the character of her subjects as affectionately and as truthfully as possible. She is unobtrusive and patient. She is a spirit catcher. She is interested for the most part in portraits of people as they are. We, on the other hand, are much more interested in allegory and narrative, not in actual character, but in dramatic personae. Not in how people really are but what they might become, or what they could stand for. Jill rarely uses falsity or distortion whereas we use it all the time: for example, the figures behind fluted glass, one perhaps threatening the other, whose faces are liquid and impressionistic, a bit like Peter Gabriel (p35). Or take the lady in the shower, her face wrenched by other hands, pulled out of shape, more in ritual than torture. This was a poster for the Lumiere & Son avant garde theatre group. Then there is the man with the football head which is more on the light hearted side and was used for a single by Ian Dury called 'Mash It Up Harry', about a little man with a big football passion, and was released, appropriately enough, during the 1998 World Cup. Last but not least is the man with balls of wool in his eyes (*Behind Closed Doors*), a not so very subtle word play on pulling the wool over your eyes, which is quite naturally what we try and do most of the time.

Gotta like what you do, otherwise it's just a chore, just a job. Especially if one is a freelance graphic designer in the UK music business – not a place to make a bundle. Like in the movie business, most workers are often out of work, and don't make a great living anyway – not starving but certainly not flush. They're in it because they like it. If it's money you want, you're better off in the estate agency business, or as a solicitor, or a dentist.

When designing, or filming, it is important to promote this 'liking', even to allow yourself to become obsessive. If you are photographing something it's that much easier to summon the motivation, and the adrenalin, if you like that something, *really* like it.

In film-making it is imperative for the director to love his characters, and his plot, and it's the same with graphic designers, at least it is with us. ◁

I say 'us' because *Like Cats And Dogs* is the fruit of three obsessions, mine, Peter's and Finlay Cowan's. Finlay's obsession was more erotic than ours, I suspect, but not by much. (He's taller, and younger.) He drew, and deeply enjoyed drawing, various arrangements of gorgeous long limbed female twins, in assorted graphic poses, and of varying nationalities (and varying degrees of undress). These twins on horseback, for example, are clearly sexual, but also psychological; naked females astride a proud stallion in front of the dark wood of the unconscious. Are they beckoning or escaping? Are they a warning?

It was clearly more interesting to extend our obsession into areas other than the erotic, not only because it was more stimulating, but also because it was more fitting for Catherine Wheel. ◁

Rob Dickinson, singer and songwriter, was obsessive

by his own admission, and contrary by nature. How about twins and animals then? Obsession alongside contrary animals, like cats and dogs. Twin obsessions, women's bodies and people's psychology. There were other connections which seemed to emerge naturally, for the cats could be Siamese (as in Siamese twins), and the dogs could be spotted, or spotty, like adolescent boys. (If we were to have girl twins then we should certainly have boy twins.) And we should have young twins, because they're even stranger, and by this time we were into an in-depth, exhaustive study of twinship. Kinship and twinship. It is, of course, identical twins we are talking here. The same but not the same. Are they telepathic? Can they share thoughts and feelings without saying them out loud? You've heard the stories; separated at birth, living apart, one suddenly feels the pain of the other across vast distances. Can one twin foresee the fate of the other? Stories of occult pacts, fierce loyalty and devotion beyond the normal. Twin sacrifices, *Twin Peaks*.

▷ When we interviewed various pairs of identical twins the experience became even more eerie. There is something both disturbing and psychedelic about being in the presence of identical twins, especially the two leggy blondes on p29. You know they're different but you keep forgetting, forever getting them confused, addressing each by the wrong name. (I must say they were so incredibly patient about this.) You think you know where you are, who is who, which is which, and then you don't. You see one sitting in front of you, and then turn round to see the same person, or so it damn well seems, coming in the door, AND HOW IS THIS POSSIBLE? It can scare the

CATHERINE WHEEL like cats and dogs

CATHERINE WHEEL "Like Cats And Dogs" CD booklet [1996]

shit out of you, especially if they decide to have a little spooky fun at your expense. And they were attractive and sexy, which simply made the whole experience more seductive and more dangerous.

▷ Yet the girls are sufficiently different for you to know the photograph opposite was not composed in the computer. They are two actual people sitting side by side, distinct yet identical. Twinly twins. But in real life the similarity is accentuated, for they move and talk identically, not just look the same! For the younger ones, and the boys on p30 in particular, the similarities were less marked, but not always, and not from certain angles. This was particularly the case with those on p31, who in some instances looked like carbon copies. That's the paranormal *X-File* type aspect in a nutshell. Are identical twins actually clones? Could they be fashioned on purpose, outside the womb, by some strange and evil device?

▷ The choice of cats and dogs seemed to nicely round off the contrasts, male and female, men and women, boys and girls, dogs and cats (little boys are made of slugs and snails and puppy dog's tails). Dogs are, of course, like blokes, ie trainable, and cats are like babes, ie uncontrollable. Dogs are loud and stupid: cats are quiet and clever. Cats are said to have a mind of their own (need I say more). It is also said that cats and dogs don't get on, but that's just hearsay.

▷ Peter provided valuable input in the selection of photos for use in the final CD booklet and was particularly adept with the graphics, perfectly matching (twinning) the typeface and layout with the images. He added thin white line boxes, redolent of scientific data (p31), sometimes on their own (as p30), sometimes 'containing' the lyrics, sometimes defocused within, and sometimes not. This elegant and not over intrusive device presented a contrast in itself – proffering a sense of containment whilst being too lightweight to really contain. The photography was executed by Tony May and Rupert Truman and the models were styled by Jackie Batten. The props for the room set (an old school house) were dutifully organised by the languid Miss Hannah Evans. The Siamese cats and graphic friendly Dalmatians were played by themselves, care of Animals Galore. The main twins in the room set were Debbie and Kelly. Room mates for the day, but womb mates for life.

0001327 | 19-2-96 | 16:13

brown 👁 green ⚖ 1.52

It's always been important to us that the extra tracks we record for singles be as good as anything we do.

Every once in a while I'll call Rob up and tell him we need to have 6 songs written and recorded by the following week. A small part of why I do it maybe a perverse need to inflict pain, the major reason is that I know it produces terrific results. The mixture of panic and a lack of time creates an unavoidable spontaneity and freedom to experiment that is unique.

The songs on our first 3 albums only tell you half the story. We hope this collection goes some way towards telling you the rest.

It's our album of non album songs.

Merck Mercuriadis

HEAL 2

It's how high you are and the time it takes to heal
It's how high you are and the time it takes to heal

I can climb a tree and push up through the leaves 'cos
Only when I try am I happier to see
My head's in some kind of space
Where boyhood used to be
It's how high you are and the time it takes to heal

But it's all a lie and I've never felt so sad
There's a streak of melancholy
Running down my back
And there's a great mistrust
That borders round the man
I call it strange from a boy who never left his head
It's how high you are and the time it takes to heal

And everyone needs someone to live by
Everyone needs someone to live by

But it's all a lie, it's a lie to make you beg
For something more
For something better than you've had
And I wish I knew
I wish I knew how to change
'Cos everyone needs someone to live by
Everyone needs someone
Everyone needs someone to live by
Everyone needs someone
It's how high you are and the time it takes to heal

Tim Friese-Greene-Hammond Organ/Piano

WISH YOU WERE HERE

So, so you think you can tell heaven from hell
Blue skies from pain
Can you tell a green field from a cold steel rail?
A smile from a veil
Do you think you can tell?

And did they get you to trade your heroes for ghosts?
Hot ashes for trees?
Hot air for a cool breeze? Cold comfort for change?
And did you exchange a walk on part in the war
For a lead-role in a cage?

How I wish, how I wish you were here
We're just two lost souls
Swimming in a fish bowl, year after year
Running over the same old ground
What have we found? The same old fears
Wish you were here

*Benoit Dunn-Pedal Steel
Mark Feltham-Harmonica
Tim Friese-Greene-Hammond Organ/Piano*

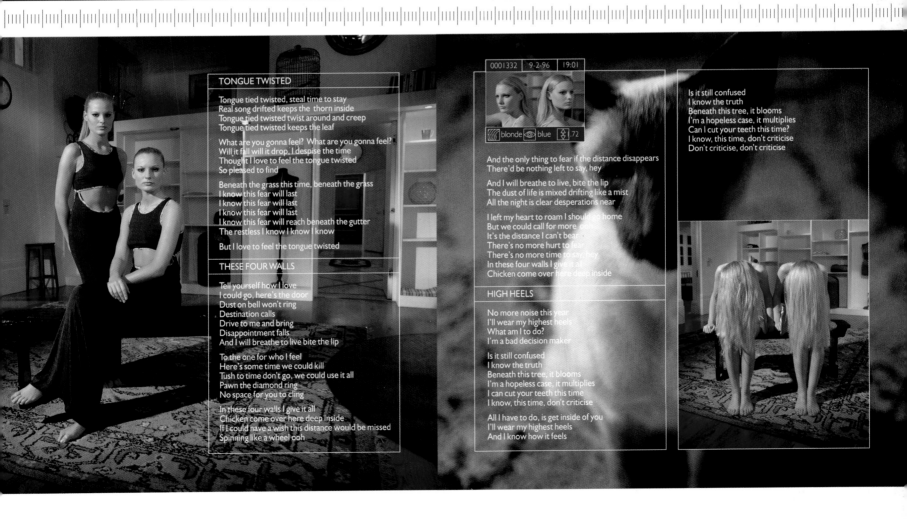

TONGUE TWISTED

Tongue tied twisted, steal time to stay
Real song drifted keeps the thorn inside
Tongue tied twisted twist around and creep
Tongue tied twisted keeps the leaf

What are you gonna feel? What are you gonna feel?
Will it fall will it drop, I despise the time
Thought I love to feel the tongue twisted
So pleased to find

Beneath the grass this time, beneath the grass
I know this fear will last
I know this fear will last
I know this fear will last
I know this fear will reach beneath the gutter
The restless I know I know I know

But I love to feel the tongue twisted

THESE FOUR WALLS

Tell yourself how I love
I could go, here's the door
Dust on bell won't ring
Destination calls
Drive to me and bring
Disappointment falls
And I will breathe to live bite the lip

To the one for who I feel
Here's some time we could kill
Tush to time don't go, we could use it all
Pawn the diamond ring
No space for you to cling

In these four walls I give it all
Chicken come over here deep inside
If I could have a wish this distance would be missed
Spinning like a wheel ooh

0001332 | 9-2-96 | 19:01

blonde 👁 blue ⚖ 1.72

And the only thing to fear if the distance disappears
There'd be nothing left to say, hey

And I will breathe to live, bite the lip
The dust of life is mixed drifting like a mist
All the night is clear desperations near

I left my heart to roam I should go home
But we could call for more ooh
It's the distance I can't bear
There's no more hurt to fear
There's no more time to say, hey
In these four walls I give it all
Chicken come over here deep inside

HIGH HEELS

No more noise this year
I'll wear my highest heels
What am I to do?
I'm a bad decision maker

Is it still confused
I know the truth
Beneath this tree, it blooms
I'm a hopeless case, it multiplies
I can cut your teeth this time
I know, this time, don't criticise

All I have to do, is get inside of you
I'll wear my highest heels
And I know how it feels

Is it still confused
I know the truth
Beneath this tree, it blooms
I'm a hopeless case, it multiplies
Can I cut your teeth this time?
I know, this time, don't criticise
Don't criticise, don't criticise

Forgive me for including one out of the cupboard, so to speak, namely a design from the good old bad old days of the Seventies, but I hear tell that the Seventies are back in fashion. Clothes, movies, northern soul, even The Bee Gees are back in vogue. (Now there's a phenomenon, those wild Bee Gees: the only recording artists to have two albums in the Top Ten

LED ZEPPELIN – IN THROUGH THE OUT DOOR

best selling albums of all time.) I never thought Led Zeppelin were either in or out of fashion. Led Zeppelin just were. ◁ This is a design I love dearly, even to this day. It tells the story of a lonely man in a dingy bar in some dreary town. The place is sparse save for a few lost souls – a failed sales rep with his jacket off, a jilted blonde in the corner, a nonchalant bartender. The joint is run down, dead on its knees. The lean, white suited guy could be a private detective on the skids, or a sleazy lawyer: a man on the run perhaps, not so much from the law as from his own past. He is burning something – a calling card, or a note telling him that he's too late, he's missed the boat. An affair too painful to recall so he is destroying the evidence to exorcise it from his mind. The whole atmosphere is jaded, dusty, from the past, sad even: a fragment from a tale untold, a frame from a 1940s movie, frozen in time, and etched in the memory. ◁ That's part of what was intended anyway. I hope some of this comes across because Peter Christopherson, Aubrey 'Po' Powell and myself, as the design team 'Hipgnosis', worked jolly hard to get this shot. Po styled it on actual New Orleans bars which he researched thoroughly and

then had recreated in a studio in West London. Peter lit the bar set exquisitely with just the right atmosphere, and I directed action and arranged composition through the lens. The sepia quality was meant to evoke a non-specific past, and to allow the brushstroke across the middle to be better rendered in colour, and so make a contrast. This selfsame brushstroke was like the swish of a wiper across a wet windscreen, like a lick of fresh paint across a faded surface, a new look to an old scene, which was what Led Zeppelin told us about their album. They also told us that the music returned to some of their old blues type roots, which was why the bar was modelled on one from New Orleans.

▷ Such an appropriate title – *In Through The Out Door* – suggesting both psychological incongruity and practical bar doors, both the paradox and the ambivalence of the main character – was he coming or going? Nobody in the bar was quite sure, even if they cared. He is a marginal character and life in the bar is marginal, caught betwixt activity and inertia, twilight characters going in through the out doors of their lives. They needed rejuvenation. A kick start. A lick of fresh paint, as per Led Zeppelin, and the music on this album.

▷ That's what they said but, being Led Zeppelin, matters didn't stop there. While it's a simple enough shot to look at – just a portrait of a man in a bar – it somehow grew in proportion and became six view points of the same man in the bar, seen by the six other characters. Six different versions of the same image and six different covers, and on the back of each was the opposite view, from the opposite side of the bar (by now the bar set was more than just a set: it was in fact a whole bar). Things didn't end there. The liner bag was printed in invisible colour ink, that is black ink which released colour when water (or spittle) was added, like some children's colouring books from the past. Finally this entire six version cover was then sold to the public in a plain brown paper bag through which you could see nothing. This ordinary looking but expensive device was in response to jibes that Led Zeppelin didn't really need a cover design at all, certainly not a detailed nor flashy one, since they would sell even in a 'brown paper bag'. Being Zeppelin they did both. As Robert Plant agreed later, it was very over the top, but then rock 'n' roll *is* over the top. "All power to pomp," he added cryptically.

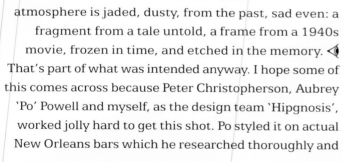

LED ZEPPELIN "In Through The Out Door" vinyl cover [1976]

PETER GABRIEL III

One particular drawback to photography for me as a designer is that it is not like painting. It does not have that 'hands on', textural quality. Photography as a medium tends to be neutral or cold: it is not a passionate technique. So I always had a hankering to produce a photograph with warm, passionate and painterly

attributes. Back in the Seventies, we at Hipgnosis often tried to get our hands between negative and print, to add a human touch to an otherwise mechanical process. We had shaded, vignetted and double exposed. We had breathed upon, and furiously rubbed, the developing print whilst it was still immersed in chemicals. We put umpteen intervening materials in the neg holder, including

stockings and grease paper to impart grain and texture to photoprints. We hand coloured, solarised and neg printed. We even experimented with 1920s glass plates hoping to smear the developing chemicals physically around the surface. All without much success.

▷ Then came our chance. Three or four events coincided. A compliant client, Peter Gabriel, a good idea (in this case a dream of melting wax effigies), an enthusiastic assistant to do the labour (Paul Maxon), but most of all a suitable technique…the manipulating of polaroids. An artist called Les Krims pioneered this technique. In deference we called them Krimsographs.

▷ Take an ordinary polaroid and as the picture begins to appear in front of you, push it around by firmly applying a blunt instrument, like a capped pen, to the polaroid surface. As the image further appears one applies more or less pressure as one requires. Since the developing chemicals are sandwiched safely between two pliable layers the pressure moves them around inside, forming the paintlike strokes you see on these pages. One is never sure precisely what will happen because one needs to apply the pressure whilst much of the image is not yet clear. But polaroids were relatively cheap so it was no great problem to do lots of them and select what was preferred. Paul then enlarged them enormously so as to further distance them from being plain ordinary polaroids.

▷ None of this would be possible without a forgiving and modest client, who was more concerned with artistic rendition than mere pop vanity. Peter Gabriel actually joined in and distorted several of the polaroids himself, which later became part of the poster overleaf. It was both funny, and economical, to utilise many of the trial attempts, cock-ups and discards. They were gathered up and placed next to each other in long rows on the floor, polaroid butting polaroid, and seemed to make a poster design right there in front of us. Various humorous comments were made, marks of approval (or cynicism) added, and further artistic embellishments imposed as the mood took. It was a real pleasure, then and now, to explore these Krimsographs, surveying them like items on display or postcards on a wall, often finding new stuff, detail and disfigurements which were previously overlooked.

▷ When we altered the colour to monochrome by simply photocopying the original polaroid in black and white negative film, and making a straightforward print, the whole ambience changed. The image on this page, which was used as part of the advertising campaign for the album, has left the realm of polaroids and has now become some weird photograph of two strange liquid figures, more like Bacon rejects, or misshapen unfortunates, like the Elephant Man, enduring some gross and incurable skin disease, skulking across open ground, heading for the safety of the shadows.

"Storm is a very funny man, and it's always fun when you first start meeting him. He has always got this box of slightly used ideas that he tries to palm you off with. Only the difficult sods get the original creative things and everyone else gets the stuff that's been rejected." PG

PETER GABRIEL "Peter Gabriel" (1978)
this page: detail // overleaf: poster

40.   *   46.   Too poetic   ✓   *   6.   Y   X

12.   BACK   Y   37 -

35. Nono Can't handle this one   20. soot Tissue   18. ₤ Nothing but fucking   Peter who?
                                                                              handle

In Verdi's Egyptian opera Aida, the heroine, Aida herself, has to face a very difficult choice. When I heard the 'Song Of Entreaty' from her father I was surprised at how the depth of his argument crystallised this invidious choice. I was **AIDA** surprised also that opera dealt so effectively with such basic yet monumental dilemmas. Falsely, and ignorantly, I had thought that though opera dealt with big issues like love and death, it was more inclined to be overblown and sentimental. Aida's father argues instead that she owes her family, her heritage, and her country many obligations, including the gathering of military information, which she could obtain, albeit deviously, from the enemy. This is eminently feasible because she is a (slave) lady in waiting at the enemy court, and because she is deeply in love with the commander of the enemy forces, and he with her. But since she is in love she cannot betray her lover, or endanger him in any way. Tricky set of issues here: tough decisions to make. Loyalty and family pulling her in one direction, passion and love pulling her in the other. Political arguments versus emotional arguments. Head against heart.

Which will she choose? And choose she must, even by default, for the enemy is about to attack her country. All around her are biased or have vested interests. So who will advise her judiciously? Family one way, friends another. It is no wonder she looks this way and then that, and then back again. ◁

The image on this page was commissioned by Scottish Opera (see more fully p100) and was produced entirely in the camera. The model (Aida) was first photographed facing left by flash to rim light the profile, and then re-exposed with slow shutter (one second) and tungsten light whilst slowly turning 180 degrees to face right,

assuming a similar 'mirror' position to how she started. She was then exposed for the third time by flash to rim light the other profile. The tungsten light was turned off for the profiles, the flash turned off for the movement. The final result is a superimposition of three separate photographs in the one frame. The tip with this procedure is to do it enough times to allow choice, since one is unsure how the movement will register visually, for it is invisible to the naked eye.

▷ Being a (graphic) tart at heart I'll work for anyone. Opera, rock 'n' roll, books and even the theatre. This portrait of a doll opposite was designed for the fringe

SCOTTISH OPERA season programme "Aida" [1998]

opposite: LUMIERE & SON "Nightfall" poster [1977]

theatre group Lumiere & Son, who produced a play – or performance piece – which was a psychological drama with wartime overtones, including a motif of war planes dropping a load of dolls at night over the inhabitants of a town, and, of course, over a few diverse characters in the play. The lighting for this moody still life of 'porcelain doll in attic corner with **NIGHTFALL** aeroplane' reflects the darkness of the action, whilst the weirdness of the characterisation is represented by the doll's expression. There is something strange about her face, I assure you. Can you see what it is?

We don't learn enough history. Big mistake. I really regret the way my secondary education enforced a choice, even before 16, between geography and history. Far too young to make a sensible decision: at that age one has not had enough history to know better, and so choose history. ◁

Rock musicians haven't learnt much from history either. Especially the rich and famous. Haven't learnt about money and how to handle it, what it does to people, especially to themselves. They are rich, but don't think about what it entails. They probably don't realise the complexity, or don't give a shit. It's not in their personal history, you see, not in their family history, only available in history at large, but that is precisely the history they don't give a flying fuck about. If they did they might manage their 'ill gotten gains' with greater skill, and even their own personalities better, which seem often to degenerate as their wealth increases. I ask you, when have you heard, or read, about a rock musician doing anything interesting with his wealth? Anything imaginative? Occasional face saving charity, but rarely anything dynamic or stimulating, nothing political, artistic or innovative. It's surprising in a way, for they seem so outspoken and flamboyant, so creative and tenacious when getting their money in the first place, as budding rock musicians, that you'd think they might show a little of the same flair in later life, but no siree! Insecurity and conservatism seep in. They start, or so it seems, to worry about earnings and ownership, lest it all slips away just as easily as it arrived. So they buy houses that are much too big for their needs, and certainly too big for their family 'culture'. And they acquire accountants and lawyers and personal secretaries, and drivers and gardeners, not to mention nannies, cars, horses or aeroplanes as obligatory side issues, and not to mention foreign property and lavish holidays. In a capitalist society you could argue that it's not their fault they got rich…but maybe it is their responsibility to handle it well and, in particular, to handle themselves well, even more now that they are so horribly rich. ◁

So Elton John has a big house, Pink Floyd have big houses, Mike Rutherford has a big house. Phil Collins has a big house (or village). Paul McCartney has more wealth than Honduras. And Mike Oldfield has a big house. Bet you thought I wasn't getting to the point. ◁

And all these folk with fucking big houses can get to believe that they are sort of different, capable of changing their mind anytime they want, changing their house or their staff if they choose, just on account of being able to pay for it.

So they can stop a project and start another one, dump commissioned work because they can easily commission alternatives, and sack a hired hand because they can simply hire another one. Because they can pay for it. They start to

MIKE OLDFIELD

EARTH MOVING

expect things and events to alter in their favour as part of normal life, as if they determine them, or own them. In a way, in our capitalist society, maybe they do. But only after a fashion. They don't really own lots of things. They don't own people or feelings, do they? They don't own the weather for Christ's sake. And they don't own artworks.

◊▷ Mike Oldfield was no different. He had a big house and thought he owned things. And one of those things was indeed my artwork. Or rather my test photographs. I was introduced to the project by Roger Dean, but the offered liaison – me and him as a design team – didn't materialise, in part because Mike was interested in a photo portrait, though not a normal one. I suggested a shot from under water, at such an angle that the underside of the water surface would act as a mirror, except for where broken by a person's head being thrust down into the water. We took a test shot of Mike himself and it worked pretty well but – here's the catch – not well enough, for it was only a test. But he liked it. Didn't want to shoot for real. But I did. He said he owned the test shoot. I said he didn't. He said he'd paid for it. I said that didn't mean he owned it (and he could have the money back if it bothered him). He said he'd have me fired. I told him to go right ahead, but he wasn't having the test photo. Some barney that. I remember being visibly shaken and, of course, expecting the worse. Not all the blame was on his head, despite his wealth, since I was probably over reactive, quick to anger and none too diplomatic, despite my not having his wealth. The upshot was that he relented and allowed us to shoot the thing properly, behaved in a restrained manner, and duly got his revenge by never speaking to me or hiring me again.

◊▷ Andy Earl and I located a five foot square glass tank, put it in a studio, secured it on a raised frame to get the camera underneath and to light it, and then filled it with tons of water. We dressed the bottom and the sides with coloured cloth, and blew bubbles from the bottom with a hose. Mike Oldfield stood at the edge of the tank on a trestle, lent over, took a deep breath and stuck his head in the water beneath the surface. Because the underside of the water was acting like a mirror one could not see any trace of him or his body outside, only his face below the surface, and the reflections of the cloth. To me he was in some fantasy world, a sort of abstract, disembodied face floating in the void, peering through a magic veil or an oily ceiling. I felt it worked well, in those pre-computer days, and the only drawback was that Mike understandably had trouble keeping his eyes open and relaxed under water.

◊▷ But not much trouble keeping his money in the bank. What I'm saying about this whole money thing is not really a sustained rational critique at all, but more a veiled request. Y'know, can Mike or Elton or any of the other guys give me or you some, as a nest egg, like? Or even for a rainy day?

MIKE OLDFIELD "Earth Moving"
vinyl cover [1989]

I know it all along – this is a family book. Good clean fun, suitable for all the family. Not. But this is a family page since Rob Dickinson of Catherine Wheel is in fact a cousin of Bruce Dickinson of Skunkworks, previously (and currently) of Iron Maiden. Rob is seen on this page adorning Catherine Wheel single bags, whilst cousin Bruce is opposite, on the back of the CD booklet for the aforesaid *Skunkworks* album. Rob looks suitably moody and sensitive, contemplative and streetwise – a set of contrary qualities for his equally contrary nature. Photography courtesy of Kevin Westenberg and Karen Lamond, graphics by Peter Curzon. ◁ Cousin Bruce on the other hand looks at first glance relatively normal, as normal as one can after a life of heavy metal and hard drinking, sword fencing, marital fencing, and umpteen days on the road. He is not, in fact, normal at all. The portrait photographs on the subsequent page are also not normal for the same reason, namely we have

used only half a face, which we have then flipped and inserted in place of the other half, and then recombined and carefully removed the join line. Bruce's face is made up of two left hand halves (or two right hand halves), and not the normal left and right halves of reality. Bruce's reality, you see, is not normal. In this instance it is too symmetrical to be real. Though the human face, even Bruce's, is said to be bilaterally symmetrical, it is not perfectly symmetrical. There is always a difference in the sides even if it is not immediately detectable. Either a sleepy eye, or a lopsided grin, odd nostrils or even different eyebrows disrupt the equilibrium. Faces are imperfect (except yours of course), and it is this side to side imperfection which lends character. In this photograph of Bruce the imperfection, this essentially human characteristic, has been temporarily suspended, and the Bruce you see here is not normal, slightly unreal, totally equal sided, more like a genetic clone or an android, just the kind of disturbing venture that Skunkworks might have initiated, in view of their alleged secrecy and alien research. This in turn is why the other elements of the design opposite and the subsequent gatefold spread exist at all. Esoteric markings, futuristic aeroplane plans, robotic hands, complex circuitry and rare photographs of aliens (actually a heavily defocused band shot) are interwoven to great effect by Peter for the inner spread of the vinyl. Dear old vinyl, the ultramodern futurist Skunkworks very secretly releases old fashioned, fondly remembered vinyl. How quaint. How alien.

CATHERINE WHEEL SINGLES

BRUCE DICKINSON SKUNKWORKS

SOLAR CON[...]

Trapped inside a web of
our needs,
Chaotic energy that sucks
All life withers in the sun
I deny what I have done
Spend my d[...]

CATHERINE WHEEL "Delicious"
CD single for the USA [1997]

The photographs opposite were rescued from album cover rejection and salvaged for a single bag for Catherine Wheel. Originally conceived for *Adam And Eve* (p79), they constituted an attempt to escape from the more formal stuff I usually do. As Rob Dickinson, vocalist for the band put it, "Free up, man. Do something less planned, not so contrived, rougher at the edges, more spontaneous. Be unlike yourself," he exhorted, "be experimental, be daring!" I nearly told him to "be gone and hire somebody else", but it was hard to resist such a bald faced challenge. So we took two actors, a photographer and a loose story about non-communication to Paris for a day out. The actors had never met before and were under strict instructions that if and when they met they were always to be in character. They had gone

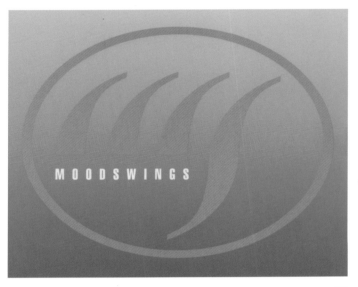

to Paris for an express and unavoidable reason – a funeral perhaps – but were not getting on at all well with each other. Each felt that it was time to finish the relationship but couldn't get to say it, especially at this juncture. They were unaware of each other's true feelings. Together but separated. ◁

Our guest photographer, Paul Postle, took pictures during the day at different locations, behaving more like a paparazzi or documentary photographer,

keeping some distance from the actors and never communicating with them directly, never posing or re-positioning them. All in all the experiment was quite diverting, extremely tiring for the actors who were in effect working all day long, except for loo breaks, and without a script as such, but the final results were unconvincing. Our story of relational dysfunction was not interesting enough as a set of stills, nor were the actors and locations visually dynamic, or strong enough in design terms for an album cover. But the day was artistically interesting as an experiment, albeit a trifle expensive.

▷ But who cares about money eh? Art is all. Money is lesser, though not according to BMG records who were concerned that the budget for the Moodswings cover (see next page) would be adhered to despite the importance, so they claimed, of the cover design, and despite the obvious complexity involved. Don't you just love it, this double speak, issuing from the mouths of record company personnel who, by and large, don't know shit? Not only because the music business as a whole is inept and unqualified – it's the only multi billion dollar business which requires absolutely no qualifications – but also because there is no known connection between sleeve design and record sales, no statistics or research which indicates any relation (at least that they would admit). If there were it would probably dictate what designs were acceptable. It was vital, they stressed, that the finished Moodswings cover was stupendous, eye catching, different and magical (all at once), and lived up to the promise of the rough sketch (see p50), but was executed for a fairly measly budget since Moodswings were not a big act, in which case why was the cover issue so important and so fraught? Anomalies and contradictions. One also suspects that these record company personnel know little about design in general, nor how specific design items work. They're unsure of what they like themselves and fearful

MOODSWINGS "Psychedelicatessen" cassette inlay [1996]

MOODSWINGS "Psychedelicatessen" CD front [1997]

of what each other might like. If I thought all this was silly enough, it was repeated several times over when it came to the 'Luminous' video, which entailed considerably greater budgetary restrictions and greater amounts of record company paranoia about the script and the lighting and the actors and the location and the editing and back again to the cost of it all. The lovable Grant and Fred of Moodswings were not, how shall I say, that cosmetically attractive and not that easy to film but I managed to do it rather badly anyway. This did not impress the record company at all. "It's a problem," they said, though I didn't understand what they meant…something about 'contemporary image'. Grant and Fred were well hidden on the album cover as you can see, or not see, and did not pose a similar 'problem'.

▷ *Psychedelicatessen* was the name of the album, which was an eclectic and amiable mixture of trance, ambient, and reggae with quasi psychedelic overtones. I can't now recall why this particular conglomerate face of faces was chosen, but the band, management and record company were in agreement (a miracle in itself). This design was concocted by Finlay and myself, based loosely, I think, on the maxim that the sum of the parts is greater than their whole, or vice versa, and that a (psyche) delicatessen is a shop full of delicacies of the psyche, not that I detect any real connection there. What is more likely is that design is one of those 'worldly' ideas wherein lies the affirmation that we are created equal; we are all of us from the same source, flowers from the same stem. We are, in effect, all one. That might be it, since 'We Are All One' is the subtitle for 'Luminous', a single from this album. In one person, or face, lies all other faces. With this in mind Finlay artfully devised a warrior type face of dignified bearing with mixed ethnic bone structure and slightly androgynous features. This design is also based on enlarged pixels or magnified dot kind of designs – step away and one sees the gross image, the large face; go closer and one starts to detect the huge number of individual or smaller constituent faces; look closer still and one sees only the individual faces, no longer aware of the larger image.

▷ You can easily guess that this artwork was a bit of a mindfuck to produce for two distinct reasons: firstly the need for facial diversity, the need to photograph lots of different faces. Expense was a factor, remember, so a lot of friends and unsuspecting but sporting passers-by were enticed off the street for a tenner a time. Secondly it was a monumental task in the computer to cut out, assemble and retouch all 400 or so individual mugshots. "The mugshot to end all mugshots," quipped Richard Manning, retoucher par excellence, showing restraint and patience beyond the normal call of duty. "And it takes a mug like me to put it all together," he added.

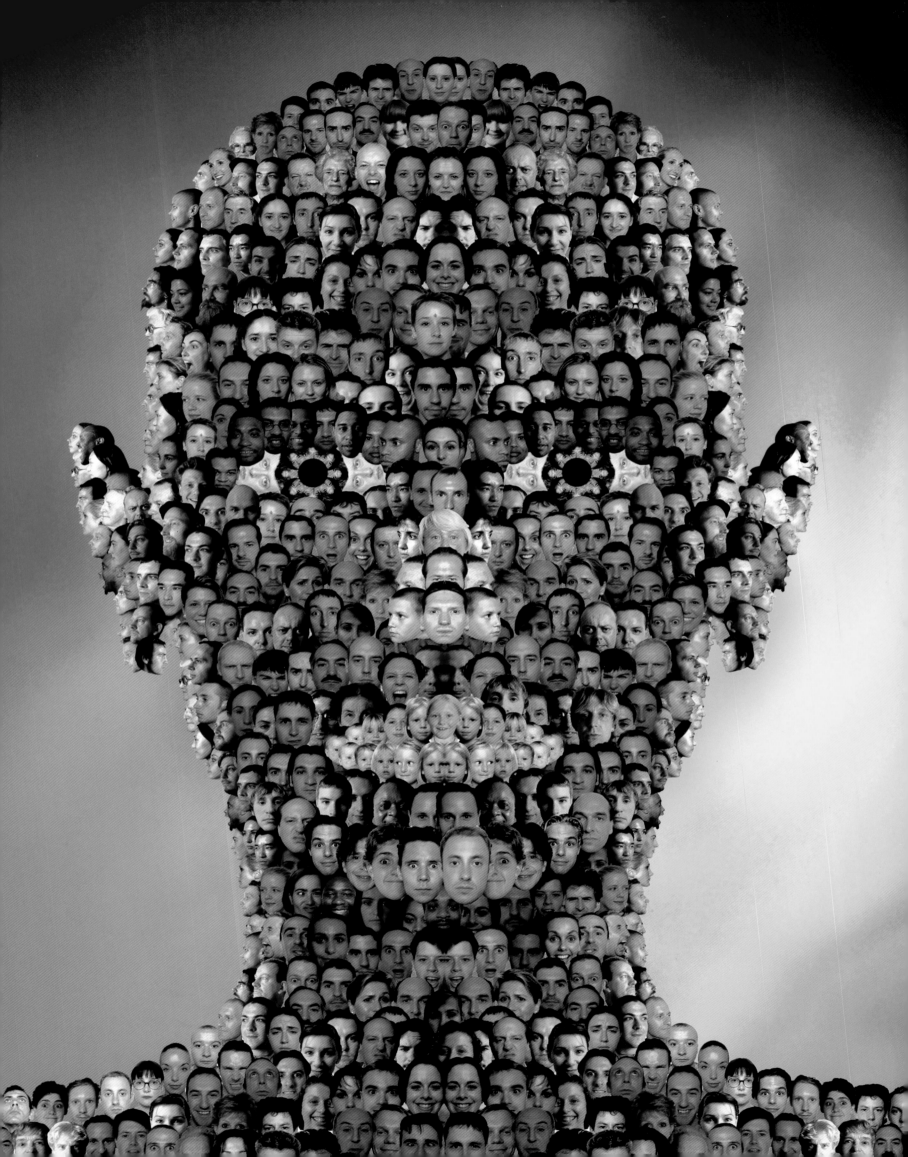

▷ Jon Crossland devised some colourful panels and elegant logo type but most
particularly came up with a unique idea for the CD booklet (and cassette), where the folds
of the concertina type booklet allowed one to play with it like a toy – a real interactive
booklet, which worked by folding over faces split in half to join up with other faces
producing incongruous variants. Top half of one face joining the bottom half of another face,
better known as the game 'consequences'. Really clever and quite original, not that anyone
from the record company, the press, or the whole wide world ever noticed it. More's the pity.

▷ In retrospect I remain unsure of this piece, undecided even as to whether I really like
it. Our honourable publishers, Sanctuary, did however, and used it for a charity project
called *Inspirations*. My cynical disposition inclines me to believe that the main inspiration
behind this was that it was free, being for a charity and all. I do know that the detail of the ear
worked well because of the gradual turning of the faces from forward to sideways at the edge.
One good turn deserves another, as they say in charitable circles.

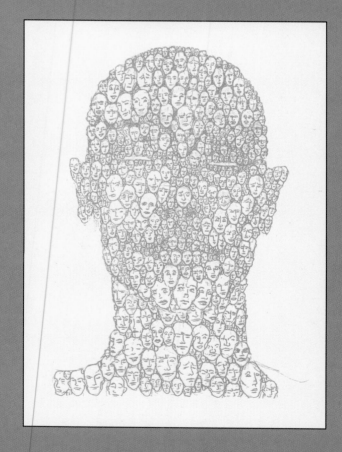

(Various) **Sculptures**

doing it for real

ELLIS BEGGS & HOWARD // HOMELANDS

Don't let anybody tell you different – rock 'n' roll is a cruel business. The advertised glamour and romance is just that, advertising. The much hyped music business is made up of much hype. For every band or artiste who makes it there are ten (or is it 50?) who do not. And for every act that makes it only one in ten (or is that 50?) survives, the rest decline in popularity all too quickly, or self combust in a welter of bickering and resentment, swept along on a tide of excess and egomania. I tell you nothing new, only to mention it in passing, and remind us that showbusiness is a heartless business, and that

representations; not likenesses of the band, but referring instead to their inner spirits. The sculptures were old but new, based upon styles derived from African, Indian and Arab sources but constructed from motorbike parts, headlamps, brass boilers, circuit wire and other bits of twentieth century cast off technology. They were planted on poles, marking the frontier, announcing loud and clear that this was their Homeland.

◗ Handsome but truculent Keith Breeden was co-opted to construct these hybrid totems. He set about building them in the bottom of his grimy and charismatic studio near Old Street, progressing in fits and starts, cobbling various unexpected elements together into barely recognisable shapes, organically wrought rather than pre-planned – at least that's how it appeared – until dramatically they came together in a flurry of creative activity, oily hands and frayed temper. I don't know to this day whether Keith really had any clear idea what he was doing, but the design he came up with was brilliantly realised. I made various amendments (in order to warrant involvement as much as to improve the outcome), but it was mostly his sculpture skills which rendered the totems majestic and unmistakable. His innate sense of what would work, whether gross shapes like the boilers, or small details like bullets for teeth, or his cannibalising of motor bike

talent is frequently and regrettably not enough on its own. My God, it should be. Circumstance and the mediocrity of popular taste propel indifferent bands to the fore and relegate others to obscurity. This seemed to be the fate of Ellis Beggs & Howard. ◖ They had one partial hit with 'No Troubles' in 1987, released an album called *Homelands* – the cover is opposite – and then seemed to fade away. I thought 'No Troubles' was great, but then what do I know? I'm in the visual department. The idea for the album design was related clearly to the title, to the fact that there were three members in the band, and that there was a dynamic mix of personalities, ethnically, spiritually and socially. I knew Nick Beggs (bass) from Kajagoogoo, for whom my film company Green Back shot a video ('The Lion's Mouth'). Austin Howard (vocals) was from Jamaica via South London, and Simon Ellis (keyboards) was from 'Up North'. The metal heads (opposite) were intended to be ethnic totems, rather than recognisable

parts, combined to make the masks characterful, humorous, and menacing – suitable as emblems for Ellis Beggs & Howard, not necessarily in that order.

◗ Photographer Andy Earl accompanied me and Tony May to Almeria in Spain to secure good light for the photograph. This turned out to be a bad idea, for the conditions were hazy, reducing contrast dramatically. It could have been shot in Brighton or the Peak District, as Keith vehemently pointed out later. Andy Earl took the band photos (on this page) at a second location, also in Spain, called Antequara, where the rock formations resemble art deco bakelite discs or piles of corn patties. The photograph for the single bag (overleaf) is also Andy's. That's young Austin (from the band) in the distance making an Aboriginal type silhouette. Keith produced the artwork and designed the background shapes, and the little ethnic logo of three figurines. All I did was have a hand in the original idea, and waffle on quite a lot.

ALAN PARSONS ⦿ ON AIR

★ *Salutary lessons* of life Number 127: when you like something a lot it's not so hard to go after it. Salutary lesson Number 13: paranoia is a great motivator. I reckon that my childhood insecurities propelled me into a conscience thing – being desperate not to disappoint, feeling every effort is worth the making. My conscience obliges me to do as much as I can, and take as many photographs as possible, so that the client will not be disappointed, and so banish me to unemployment. This partly explains a load of hot air balloons which I orchestrated for Alan Parsons' album entitled *On Air*, which in turn meant getting up very early on several mornings and racing round the countryside chasing balloons, or waiting patiently for balloons to appear over the horizon and praying that they would come our way, or peering through the early morning mist to see if balloons had even taken off (or if they'd been grounded by adverse conditions), or craning our necks upwards to photograph the underside, or driving madly round country lanes in the dwindling light to get that one great moody sunset shot, or dashing between sundry balloons taking off en masse, tripping over guy ropes, being singed by hot gas blasts, told off by balloon stewards, and so on and so forth. All of this frenetic

opposite:

ELLIS BEGGS & HOWARD "Where Did Tomorrow Go?"

single bag front [1989]

endeavour was fuelled by my liking hot air balloons. I didn't get to go in one because I was too busy photographing the bastards, but I got to enjoy them immensely. There is something very particular about them, floating gracefully and silently for the most part, except for the intermittent burst of the hot air cylinder – an unmistakable sound – as they glide serenely over tree tops, and sweep across fields like gigantic airborne baskets suspended on the breeze. They come in vivid colours, vibrant stripes and graphic designs, also in a variety of shapes, some truly bizarre, some grandly commercial. It must be hard to resist putting on corporate logos and company names (highly visible airborne advertising), but I prefer the standard balloon shape as in the CD label on this page, with vertical pleats and bright colours.

▷ I like air balloons or else I would not have been able to do this album cover design…that's my point. The picture overleaf, for example, of the stellate pattern is actually composed of the underside of several balloons photographed on four different occasions. The balloon in the never ending wood (p58) took two photosessions. The aeroplanes were photographed at two different air shows, one in the UK, one in the US, whilst the main design, the front cover on p57, consists of another day's photosession (in Wiltshire) plus of course a very costly balloon. I used five different photographers (thank you Paul Maxon, Tony May, Alton Omer, Rupert Truman and myself) on at least ten different occasions, in sundry locations, as well as library shots, courtesy of Adrian Smith, of the stupendous mega balloon festival in Albuquerque New Mexico, when 800 or so balloons congregate watched by over a million people. What a sight! Two retouchers were involved (thank you Richard Manning and Jason Reddy), one model maker, one graphic designer (thank you Peter Curzon) and several occasional assistants including Jody January and Julien Mills. After that lot it's no wonder I didn't make an enormous profit, but I did get to see some fantastic balloons.

ON AIR

ALAN PARSONS "On Air" CD booklet [1996]
previous page: CD front

ALAN PARSONS ON AIR
CD ROM • FOR COMPUTER USE ONLY

5300099

BIEM/STEMRA

WARNING: PLAYING ON AUDIO CD PLAYERS MAY CAUSE DAMAGE TO EQUIPMENT

Recommended System Requirements:

PC/Windows • 486DX 33Mhz or better • At least 8MB of RAM • Microsoft Windows 3.1 or later • Double speed CD ROM drive • Colour monitor and video card supporting 256 colours at 640x480 • 16 bit sound card (Soundblaster 16 or compatible) • Mouse

Macintosh • Colour capable Macintosh computer • At least 8MB RAM System software 7.0.1 or later • Double-speed CD ROM drive Colour monitor supporting 256 colours • Mouse

COMPACT disc

The jet aeroplanes on the CD label here were also one of the most awe inspiring things I've ever witnessed. These were Red Arrows. Their formation flying routine is completely terrifying and the precision truly mind boggling. There was one moment when two groups of three jets hurtled directly at each other at 600 mph a few hundred feet above the ground and scared the shit out of me. Time stood still in the face of calamity. ◁

Equally stupendous, but in a completely different way, was the main shoot (p57). The weather was perfect (scudding clouds and blue skies), the balloon was beautifully made (thank you John Lewis), and the hilltop location was neat, nicely rounded and very mystical. Perhaps it was a burial mound, or a natural beacon, a junction point on the criss cross ley lines of Wiltshire. And such a cute idea (or so I

thought) – this balloon in stately flight, on air (as per title). A light bulb balloon, correctly balloon shaped, but representative of the idea of flight, hovering literally and metaphorically above a head shaped mound. The outline of a head with a light bulb above it. The symbolising of an idea…the idea of flight…whilst in flight.

▷ Which is what the very tall Alan Parsons told me was the theme of his album. It was the idea of flight, the ambition to fly, which propelled man into the air, he said, far above me, as if part of him had already been there. So he should know, right?

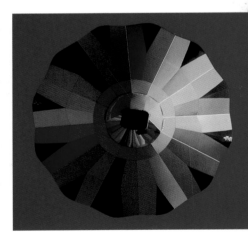

Well, phuck Phish, that's what I say now. All was laughter then, but it turned to tears. Everybody was keen to work at first, compliments flying everywhere. We submitted a load of rough ideas, which they said they loved. They chose one. We went for it. They said that's splendid. It was used on the finished record. All seemed fine and dandy, and then we never heard from them again. Not a word, not a whisper. Zilch. A deafening silence, despite much talk about working together on the next (studio) album, and that this live album job was a sort of courtship, a trial period, a getting to know each other, with a long term relationship in the offing, because such relations tend to work well (Pink Floyd, Catherine Wheel) and it's what Phish wanted anyway, and so on and so forth.

abcdefghijklmnopqrstuvwxyz1234567890

opposite:

PHISH "Slip Stitch And Pass" CD front [1997]

I was impressed back then by their live show because Phish were clearly intent on playing music (not going through the motions), keen to improvise and adapt (within context), and to extend songs and pieces in unexpected ways. I was even more impressed to learn later that they did not have a set list. Good grief, no set list! When playing live they had little idea what they were going to perform until they were on stage in front of an audience. How about that for daring? Phish had built up a reasonably large and faithful audience across the States, not unlike The Grateful Dead many moons ago, and every time fans came they would experience something a little different. They would be escorted on a different (audio) journey which, considering the laws of average, might not always be that enjoyable. But the overall approach was always refreshing and paid off more times than not. When finally we met face to face it felt very promising. And they gave me a little present of a book entitled *The Perfect Storm*. Excellent! ◁◉

The design selected (see previous page) featured a man running down a beach holding a piece of yarn (could be wool, string, or rope) which he was pulling from a giant ball beyond. This humongous ball of wool (or yarn or string) was intended, in a loose kind of way, to represent the music that the musician, the figure on the beach, was unravelling. The wool was the theme or melody line, which the musician would tease out, running with it until the extensions and variations were exhausted, the music was over, and the giant ball fully unwound.

The image was a poetic attempt to represent improvisation. The running man holds the end of the yarn like a relay baton, ready to pass it on to other musicians who could continue to run with it, in the same way as Phish and jazz groups do with their music. The shadows in this image keep the runner anonymous, for he is representative of any and all musicians. They also lend weight to the giant ball, and give added reality to all the elements, particularly the wavy yarn. Where will the running man go? How far down the beach? How extended an improvisation? How long is a piece of string? ◁◉

What upsets me about the Phish episode, why I say "phuck Phish" in such a childish fashion, is that the Phish didn't bite. To reflect the homespun individualistic mood of the music, Jon Crossland converted his own handwriting into a unique custom made font, called 'Phish Face', ho hum, that was used throughout the design. He also added some very nice computer collages, textural additions, and negative solarisations to the whole package, but Phish didn't bite. They said they liked the cover, but they didn't come back. Of course no client in a capitalistic society is obligated to return to their supplier. Phish can do, and did, just whatever they want. But the central feature was ignored, ie a long term relationship, which had been clearly aired and was an additional reason for all of us to work together. One outing is rarely enough to judge and the value of a longer relationship depends upon weathering the storm, in all senses of the word, so that lines of communication (artistic, business and electronic) are improved. In addition, nobody said a fucking word about it. Phish never spoke to us afterwards, never intimated disappointment, or offered a critique. The giant ball of wool was an expensive proposition, of course, but nobody wanted to pay for it. Despite early artistic agreement there was protracted financial disagreement. The shortfall meant that the giant ball of wool was not quite as giant as desired.

▷ And the moral of this woolly tale is…don't be stingy, guys, not with the money (false economy), not with your belief (in your choice), and not with the communication (design is a two way deal), especially criticism. I don't actively like criticism but I need it, otherwise I might not get better. So fishy Phish, wherever you are, speak with me don't phuck with me. Album covers and love are better the second time around.

Phish

over 73 minutes
of phish recorded
live in hamburg,
germany in 1997 —
includes several
unreleased concert
favorites

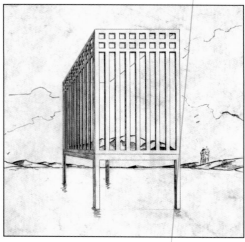

Come closer, I'd like to whisper. I wish to talk about a cock-up – too strong a word – a partial failure then. I need to whisper because failing, partially or not, is frowned upon generally speaking: in Japan it could be the second most appalling admission after shame. In America failure is similar to depression, or the negative aspects of life, usually swept aside under the proverbial carpet. In graphic design circles failing is not such a popular word either. The closest designers normally get to it is the expression 'it doesn't work for me', implying the possibility that it might work for someone else, so it's not so bad after all. And to put it in a book…◀

This design of a baby's giant cot standing near a river (river of life no doubt), in the verdant countryside but amidst leafless trees, with an adult figure blurred in the background, escaping presumably from the confines of his cot (the confines of his youth), does not work so well for me, as they say. It's a bit of a mess. It fails because firstly the idea is a bit obvious perhaps. Secondly because the realisation is impaired. If it were contradictory scale I was after – big cot, little figure – then the cot needed to have been much bigger, high as a tree, imposing like castle turrets. And if the structure was intended to be elegant, well proportioned, or finely crafted then we should have designed it better. And if the location was intended to be evocative, then plain to see, it isn't. And if the lighting was supposed to be dramatic then we should have chosen a better day.

▷ None of these considerations is completely awful: just not great enough on their own, or preferably in combination, to elevate a very moderate idea into an arresting image. It is true that we had bad luck, insufficient funds, poor weather, too many principles (we could have enlarged the cot further in the computer) and so on and so forth. But who cares? Who wants to know about difficulties and adverse circumstances if they degrade the final outcome? Who needs excuses? Not the reader, not the client. And therefore not the designer.

▷ Now the alternative, or secondary image (see overleaf), works much better, I think. Here one is not so interested in the size or the detailed design of the cot, but in the perspective. The struts, which are a little boring from the front, are here dynamic and pull the eye down to the figure in the bed, clearly now an adult in child mode, trapped in his own infancy, screaming to be let out. It's only his own

CATHERINE WHEEL *happy days*

aversion to growing up which keeps him a prisoner. But he's still a child at heart so has a tantrum, shakes his rattle and screams his head off. Even the lighting was more kind that day, providing dramatic moulding to a dramatic subject.

▷ This version was used as the front cover in the UK against our wishes, but with completely the wrong crop, not like you see here at all. Which is why it is here, and why the one opposite is here, cock-up or not – one to permit the other.

▷ PS The real irony about this story is that this design was, I have to confess, initially conceived for Pink Floyd, for a film to accompany the song 'Hey You' on their 1994 world tour. A moving cot is a different kettle, as they say in filmland, but the image was appropriated by Catherine Wheel, and is forever theirs. To balance matters the tree head ('Tree Of Half Life' p115) was appropriated by the Floyd and is forever theirs, though originally conceived for…Catherine Wheel. Cat's out of the bag now. But then again the initial version of *Dark Side* was designed for someone else. As they say in the legal business, and like I should know, ownership is 9/10 of the law.

Glam rock, hard rock, heavy metal, thrash…what is it with these groups that they invariably choose names of fantasy (Whitesnake, Aerosmith, Mötley Crüe), darkness (Led Zeppelin, Iron Maiden, Judas Priest), or horror (Megadeth, Poison and Anthrax)? Think about it. Anthrax itself is truly horrible. Germ warfare. A powerful biological weapon that causes extreme pain, disfigurement and death. A litre of anthrax would decimate Guatemala. Yet a nicer bunch of guys you couldn't hope to meet. Well, as far as I could tell on the phone from the States, and later in LA for a couple of meetings. I'm not an enormous fan of heavy metal (or hard rock or thrash etc), but I liked this album *Stomp 442*. It had an interesting minimal quality, a pared down heavy metal, like to its bare bones. Lent it an edge, an air of incongruous purity. We suggested, amongst other things, something equally minimal and direct, a giant ball of heavy metal. That was it. A humongous ball of twisted metal, sitting there, bold as day, upfront, no messing, like the music (see next page). Anthrax liked it but were doubtful of its prospective reality: "Would it be convincing?" they asked. I assured them that my normal policy was to 'do it for real'. They remained sceptical, but I told them blithely that this was the way I had done it for years, and it had seemed, by and large, to work. Charlie, Anthrax drummer and design rep, happened to be an avid Led Zeppelin fan and he said okay, fine, in that engaging drummer way – hmm, if that's cool, dude, then go for it. ◀ The image overleaf is a real, tall, giant ball of metal car parts – look closely and you'll identify fenders, cylinder heads, engine blocks, side panels etc, etc – whose size can be gauged by the figure standing alongside, and also by the size of the parts themselves, for they are all taken from actual scrap American cars (because Anthrax are American). I remember this manager type person being amazed, disbelief written across his financial features. "Round as a ball," he commented astutely. (Can you guess how this junk ball has actually been put together?) ◀ My fantasy for the ball was as follows: it was held together by mental energy, exerted by the

ANTHRAX *STOMP 442*

native figure standing alongside. It was his ball, his personal weapon, his ally, his pet metal crusher. He didn't need electronic controlling devices, any more than he needed protective gear, fancy clothing, or even a suit. He didn't suffer bodily variations, countering them instead with pure thought waves. His metal ball could easily roll anywhere, across anything, crushing things in its path, absorbing unto itself new bits when necessary, replenishing as it destroyed. The figure had mentally summoned it to heel, like an obedient dog, before issuing it with fresh instructions. If this narrative fails to appeal, then it remains just as it started, a fucking great ball of heavy metal.

▷ The principal location was a bizarre scrap yard in East London near the docks, part of an electrical complex (Beckton) which included a power station, turbine houses and large sheds now falling into disrepair, crumbling majestically, precursors of a nuclear future. Stanley Kubrick had used the yard previously, unknown to us of course, for a Vietnam movie called *Full Metal Jacket*, and I fondly imagined he chose it for the same reasons. Which in fact was not the case, since he had blown everything up himself for the movie. Art imitates life, they say, but life imitates art, says Kubrick.

▷ Peter deployed various photos of the location to great effect in the CD booklet (overleaf), including some strange machinery from the scrap yard itself, adding a solarised effect of his own to enhance the futurist metal hell quality, then darkening them to allow lyrics to be reversed out white. He used sections of building, plus superimposed fire, for the back cover (this page) and a textural close-up for the CD label (see p72). Tony and Rupert were the ever reliable, much abused, photographic team, and used a Hasselblad with a 60mm wide lens and daylight Ektachrome.

FUELED

I'm out to mix it up and change my complexion
To coat the feelings and cure my depression
A shot of petrol is my bonafide method
To lose control and get thoroughly distracted

I'm on the money, here I come
Fuel for my engine, and I'm gone

I like to forget why I feel this compulsive
As I toss tomorrow's dreams in the garbage
What's important is a mind that's sicker
Turning Jekyll into Hyde much quicker

I'm on the money, here I come
Fuel for my engine, and I'm gone

1,2,3,4,1,2,3,4
Kickstart and turn me over
Punchdrunk, but I'm still sober
Fourteen years and a whole lot bolder
And I don't flinch
Hungry and I'll take the best
'Cause I never wanted anything less
What doesn't kill me makes me stronger

1,2,3,4, I can't close my broken door
It's just the nature of the way things work
You wanna do it give a damn
Anyone can do it but it takes a man not to
Try so hard to give me a real life
Anyone can do it but it takes a man not to
It's just the nature of the way things work

I'm like a beat inside you, a drug you steal
Two sides of the coin that I've been blessed with both
Or one hand I am you, but I don't like you
I guess that's the nature of the way things work

I'm on the money, here I come
Fuel for my engine, here I come

1,2,3,4,1,2,3,4
Kickstart and turn me over
Punchdrunk, but I'm still sober
Buko dadd son my shoulder
With much to think
Hungry and I'll take the best
'Cause I never wanted anything less
What doesn't kill me makes me stronger
It's like a war inside, no, a throne, as I know
Tell me it's suicide, tell me something I don't know

I don't know why I've been made some kind of hero
When I've done all I can do to prove I'm not
It's amazing to think someone could trust me
Tell me what do you know about me really?
And if you make the mistake of getting close to,
Me, you'll just give me all that you've got
So I don't know why I've been made some kind of hero
When I've done all I can do to prove I'm not

1,2,3,4,1,2,3,4
Kickstart and turn me over
Punchdrunk, but I'm still sober
Fourteen years and a whole lot bolder
And I don't flinch
Hungry and I'll take the best
'Cause I never wanted anything less
What doesn't kill me makes me stronger

KING SIZE

I want to be part of the program
I want to be part of the whole damn thing
I say, minimum effort, maximum gain
From the inside out it all looks the same
Making me feel stronger
Making me feel like The Hulk I'll be
King Size

Here it is,
I'll stake my claim and I'll be first to warn you
Here it is,
I think the devil lives in California

Check out the freak I'm laughing
Excuse me are you talking to me?
I say, minimum effort, maximum gain
From the inside out it all looks the same
Making me feel harder

Making me feel like The Hulk I'll be
King Size
Here it is,
I'll stake my claim and I'll be first to warn you
Here it is,
I think the devil lives in California

I'm on a mission, I'm on a mission
For my survival, my king size position,
I'm on a mission, in my condition
Outside my world I know there's
No place like home
I'm on a mission, my king size position
Outside my world I know there's
No place like home
I can't stop my life from crashing
Out of control, I'm out of control
Nothing to fear but fear itself and me

I, I'd never sell my soul
I never did a god damn thing 'cause
I'd never tell my soul for something that's free
Minimum effort, maximum gain
From the inside out it all looks the same
Nothing to fear but fear itself and,
Nothing to fear but fear itself and,
Check out the freak and I'm still laughing
Nothing to fear but fear itself and me

Here it is,
I'll stake my claim and I'll be first to warn you
Here it is,
I think the devil lives in California

Main Solo: Dimebag
Lyrical Assist: Rich Ross

AMERICAN POMPEII

I try to imagine the best place I've been
Can I go back again?
Open my eyes, what was no longer exists,
I can't go back again
I like to pretend that nothing has changed
And never went too far
But it started to lose me like a four-hour movie
I'd already seen
Holding onto my memory of what this used to be
Holding onto my memory of you

Sometimes I tell myself that things are O.K.
Another lie but it makes me feel better
Never as old as I was today
I'm gonna breakdown

In American Pompeii
In American Pompeii
Break myself just to live this way
Never as old, as I was today
American Pompeii

Look in my eyes and see how sick I feel
About what you've become
Filthy and twisted like you never existed
I know what you were
Your beauty forgotten under mountains of schism
I don't wanted return
Giving up my memory of what this used to be
Giving up my memory of you

Sometimes I tell myself that things are O.K.
Another lie but it makes me feel better
Never as old as I was today
I'm gonna breakdown

In American Pompeii
In American Pompeii
Break myself just to live this way
Never as old, as I was today
American Pompeii

Try to imagine the best place I've been
Can I go back again
Open my eyes it just no longer exists
I can't go back again
I'm giving up my memory of what this used to be
Giving up my memory of you

Main Solo: Charlie
Solo Tag: Mike Tempesta
Shaker: Scott
Bongos: Charlie

PS *At the time of writing Stanley Kubrick has just died. It may be out of place but I'd like to say that I admired him greatly, not just for Clockwork or Strangelove but most particularly for 2001 which blew me and my friends away back in 1968 when we watched in awe as the black obelisk careered through space, cradling our thermos of tea and a handful of pre rolled joints. God speed, Stanley, to Jupiter and beyond.*

opposite:

ANTHRAX "Stomp 442"
CD front [1995]

ANTHRAX STOMP 442

▷ Did you guess how this ball structure was produced? Or did you feel indifferent? Or that to know would decrease the effect, like learning a sport result before seeing the game, or the murderer during a whodunnit before seeing who done it? I'm going to tell you anyway, because I thought it was kind of neat. Think of a ball or sphere. Picture its volume in your mind. For a start you cannot see the back half of the ball from wherever you look. Secondly, you cannot see inside if the surface is solid, ie opaque. Thus half a hollow ball is all you ever need. Now a sphere, or a semi-sphere, is equal and regular, therefore any one section, or quadrant say, is the same shape and curvature as any other, and this is the key. We, or rather Model Solutions, built one hollow quarter of one half of a ball. And that was tough enough, finding the car parts, and cutting and welding, twisting and joining them all together, much of it on site. They then hoisted the quarter 'shell' by crane into four positions appropriate for each quadrant of a complete circle, such that the lighting and the perspective would be correctly maintained. We photographed these four separate positions and joined the shots via computer. And because the quadrant is so busy to look at, full of assorted shapes, different colours and varying textures, you cannot tell that it's the same piece that has been rotated. Neat, huh? When retouching we doctored a few of the more prominent bits to make it impossible to detect any similarity. The end composite is in fact a real full size ball simply not existing all at the same time. It took one day to build, one day for shooting, and several years off our lives.

ANTHRAX *STOMP 442*

They promised us a better life. They said They would
look after us and help us. All we had to do was listen to
Them once a week. And it came to pass that They were
right. The people were happier, more protected, and
we felt a greater sense of security and inner peace. We
were emotionally more stable, accommodating more
easily our psychological demons. And of course we
listened once a week. Most important was to follow
Their advice for infant and child-care. Children clearly
benefit from secure surroundings. One of the aids to
infant security was a personal pet, a soft toy,
preferably a teddy bear. To this end They kindly
donated a teddy bear to every child. A very ordinary
looking teddy, but one all kids seemed to adore. It was
strangely durable; resistant to unthreading, but
otherwise normal. Then one day teddy caught fire, and
as his fur was eaten away by the flames, it revealed a
mechanical interior, metal frame, wires, capacitors
and micro chips replete with power unit and circuitry.
Teddy was in fact a robot. It was also a transmitter and
receiver, capable of maintaining constant
surveillance. More insidious were aerosol sedatives,
sonar mantras below audible range, and, if needs
must, audio visual hypnotic capacities and brain wave
simulators. No wonder teddy helped foster security,
programming our children from an early age.
Conditioning not comforting. When we became adult
citizens all we needed was a subliminal trigger to keep
us docile AND content. Listen once a week, that's all,
They said. That's all that was required to keep us in
line. So much for the promises They made.

THE CRANBERRIES "Promises" CD single [1999]

"Promises"

BLINKER THE STAR "August Everywhere" CD front [1999]

been difficult to fake, especially the small ones in the neck, and the even smaller one in the head itself, and secondly because the quality of light between sculpture and background, particularly in the shadows, would have been tricky to keep consistent.

▷ The staging of the real event possessed a poignancy not initially anticipated. The ice swan was always going to die, inexorably, inevitably, sadly melting away in the desert heat. It lived beautifully for a short while before losing its shape and its soul. A phoenix in reverse, turning into water in order to replenish the parched earth beneath: a noble but pathetic gesture, for it was only a drop in an ocean of dryness. This sadness stayed with me, along with the irony of a clearly impermanent event

Blinker The Star
August Everywhere

There's a wave of heat that comes through Death Valley, California, in the summer afternoon that is like a massive boxing glove. You step out of the car and wham, the heat smacks you in the face, and pushes you back against the car. Extraordinary! The temperature is already 110°/120° and then at about 4pm it quickly rises another 10° or 20°, not to mention the heat coming off

the desert floor. Good place for an ice sculpture eh? ◁

Fears of immediate melt were in fact exaggerated because although the ice swan (opposite) is, of course, melting steadily, it does so only at the thinnest points, such as the wing tips and, unfortunately, the slender necks, which kept breaking as the swans were carried out of the ice truck, which was leaking anyway and which wouldn't keep below freezing, which is kind of desirable when dealing with ice sculptures. Then there were bumpy roads to contend with, and a puncture in the middle of a treeless nowhere with no jack, and always the heat, the intense heat. ◁

Notwithstanding this catalogue of misfortune the temptation to comp this design in the computer was resisted (just) and I was so glad. Firstly because the myriad subtle reflections of the arid scenery would have

made permanent by capturing it in the camera.

▷ What also stayed with me was the incandescent light bouncing around inside the ice sculpture, so bright that the camera aperture had to be stopped down, turning the midday scene into a night-time one. What also stayed was the memory of Gus, the ice sculptor, over 60 but ever resourceful and charming in the face of adversity, and one Jordon Zadorozny, aka Blinker The Star, who came along on the shoot and was both friendly and helpful. He comes from Canada: two days in Death Valley was probably enough, let alone putting up with my belligerence and impatience at leaky ice trucks, neck breaking swans, punctures in the desert and what have you. I wonder still what he made of the whole experience and hope he enjoys his cover design as much as we do.

▷ This 'we' is the royal we. Jon Crossland thought of an ice sculpture (for a previous Blinker title 'Heaven For Now'), I envisaged the swan as a symbol of the muse, and went on location with photographer Rupert Truman, and Peter Curzon did all the graphics.

A portentous title perhaps for a hard drinking, hard driving bunch of hard geezers, but who are we to judge? It goes to show that rock musicians are not as bone headed as one might believe or as shallow as the media might allege. I've lost our favourite idea for this cover but I recall that it was a double image, an amalgam of two opposites, a baby and a ghoul I think, and the viewer tended to see one or the other not both at the same time. I remember that the record company (EMI) thought this design too evil; it would put off prospective punters. Hard rock, hard drinking punters upset by a little old design; I think not. But the band, Thunder by name, but not by nature, went along with this view, skilfully guided by their far sighted but short haired manager, who seemed continually to consign them to mediocrity and under achievement. (Only my opinion, of course, and a pretty cheap one at that.) If anything, I think my anger is related more to my liking the chaps and then separating from them. They were always friendly and straight. We did several jobs together (including the excellent frog on p179), but by and large we jointly arrived at the wrong solutions, and in the end I got fired: not, I think, because we didn't get on, but

THUNDER LAUGHING ON JUDGEMENT DAY

opposite: THUNDER "Laughing On Judgement Day" vinyl front [1992]

because the manager deemed it better for their career. What did his band want with an old fart designer anyway? Perhaps I was losing my touch, which is a really scary thought for artists. Burn out. Yesterday's news. Past one's sell-by date. It doesn't help the old insecurity networks to be working in a young person's business, transient and ephemeral by nature, fashion orientated, mainly run by unqualified and fearful middle managers, and populated largely by charlatans, stupid people and ruthless fuckers, the latter furiously trying to promote anaesthetised product, while the musicians themselves are frequently an assortment of egomaniac crazies driven by deep seated insecurity and avarice. But I obviously love it really, having remained in it for 30 years…slagging it off is a perk of maturity, and must be fiercely defended, since there are very few other advantages to age. ◁

Where was I? Oh yes, Thunder, and our see-saw relationship. In order for a judgement to be made there must be two sides to an issue (at least), hence two sides to the front cover design (p75). A right and left side. An interior and an exterior. These are divided by He Who Judges, namely a hard, metal encrusted figure who is clearly screaming, or laughing, madly. At some moment in all our lives there comes a judgement day (so it is written), and time is therefore a crucial element, hence the clock on the wall, and all the sundry clock parts in the floor. The

teeth are made of rocks (as in rock music), and the iron bust is supported by bottles of booze (as also in rock music, ho ho). The sun of bananas echoes the head of the stomping figure (p74), another rejected rough based on Max Ernst's 'Fireside Angel', whilst the repeating mouth – the echoing hollow laughter of Lucifer on the day of judgement – is reminiscent of an advert we designed back at Hipgnosis for Syd Barrett 18 centuries ago. Mouths within mouths, wheels within wheels.

▷ The sculpture was made by Keith Breeden on the windswept hills of Llanfihangel in Wales. Since he made it in between house building, having a baby and living in a caravan, the anguished expression probably represented the inner state of Keith's mind fairly accurately. We put the whole thing together on a Quantel Paintbox computer system. Some of it worked okay (the clock tiles), some of it didn't (the differing left and right panels). An odd mixture, an odd experience. It was Keith's last stand in the cover design business (barring guest appearances on *Chrome* and *Division Bell*) and it was sad to lose him from the fraternity. He did great stuff. That's him standing on the rocky outcrop, staff in hand, his mystic cloak swept up behind him by a gust of wind. A sentinel, surveying his kingdom. A mad monk watching over his flock. A lonely figure, a man of destiny. What twaddle. Keith Breeden is an honest man and a fine designer, but about as mystic as my left nipple.

(Human) Bodies

frightened by meaning

Rick Wright
Catherine Wheel
Thunder
Godley And Creme
Scorpions

Crash Helmet Angel

RICK WRIGHT "Broken China" CD booklet

ɸ above: front cover / right: back cover [1996]

Bear with me for the following anecdote which will, I hope, affirm the value of long term design relationships. The difficult set of events which transpired would not have been tolerable, would not have been overcome, except for the relationship between us and Catherine Wheel. This relationship, like that of Pink Floyd, endured because of mutual respect and has provided for much good work and, I'd like to think, mutual stimulation. The design in question (p81) for the US album cover consisted of several naked people squashed awkwardly into open wooden boxes, a bit like postal sorting boxes, or enormous pigeon holes. The idea behind it was about contrary feelings (or opposites), which were a known and creatively useful characteristic of the songs, and of the personality of lead vocalist Rob Dickinson. This contrariness is embodied here as a kind of 'elegant contortion', where bodies are crammed as prettily as possible into confined spaces. The people in the boxes are separate in their pigeon holes, but together in the rows of shelves, adjacent but apart. We are all alone living in our separate compartments, trapped in our own personalities, yet trying hard to be together and share our destinies. This design is a vehicle for these ideas. The nude people are constrained, but only metaphorically, for the 'boxes' are open and the people could easily get out. This design is not about imprisonment or torture, but about the illusion and the sensation of separateness whilst together. ◁

The theme of contrariness is illustrated as much by the form of this image as by the intellectual content. The body shapes are soft and curvaceous, but the shelves are hard and straight. The contours of the people are flowing and irregular whilst those of the boxes are rigid and regular. The bodies are organic but the boxes are manufactured. I always felt that this design owed much to Art Nouveau, more clearly illustrated by the rough sketch (p80), wherein natural organic lines and shapes are contained by

CATHERINE WHEEL

sympathetic borders, but in our case by harsh and graphic rectangles in order to indicate the harder sides of the music. The main image is a real event staged in a studio in Chalk Farm, London. The boxes were specially constructed, placed in rows as you see, and the hapless models persuaded to get in as best they could. They needed little direction, as it happened, since the size of the boxes forced them to adopt the requisite positions. Tony May and Rupert Truman took the photograph. The end design is a record of bits of reality, just not all occurring at the same moment, and not necessarily the right way up.

▷ What is more to the point is what happened next.

▷ Catherine Wheel felt that their UK (but not US) record label was not treating them well and so decided, I think with good reason, to change to another record label. This was quite a difficult and painful procedure, legally and emotionally, at least as far as I could discern from the manager (Merck Mercuriadis). It's gotta be done, he confided, but it's very difficult. The effects on the design department (that's us) might not have been very noticeable except that the aforesaid manager felt that it was appropriate, and artistically desirable, to change the cover design. He wanted us to alter the arrangement, or the colour, or the layout of the US cover (p81/82) or any combination

ADAM *and* EVE

thereof, for the UK cover, even though it had already been released to the public. We are not averse to alternative versions in different territories (or for different formats), but we're only prepared to endorse them for design reasons, or in the face of indecision (too many nice photos to choose from), or, I guess, for huge amounts of money if it comes to the crunch. Actually I'm joking, but the smile was soon wiped off my face. Owing to our affection, respect,

and long relationship, we reluctantly acceded to the request for change and made some alterations, but on the clear understanding that such 'new' versions were only usable if they were superior. One of these versions was in green and used only four boxes (p82). It was okay but substituted the crowded 'boxed in' feeling of the US or red version with a graphic approach. Whereas the red version was 'self contained' and 'emotionally crowded', the green version was cool and spacey. It was clearly

CATHERINE WHEEL "Adam And Eve" US CD front [1997]

different but – and here's the rub – it was not necessarily better.

▷ We had several meetings with Merck and singer Rob Dickinson to express our misgivings about the whole exercise, both in principle, and in specific. But no agreement was forthcoming. The situation slowly and inexorably deteriorated. Phone calls became awkward, angry and threatening. Merck remained adamant. I became entrenched. I could not (legally) fight the issue, partly because I didn't have the clout, and also because I really didn't want to obstruct the progress of a band I admired. I resigned, and took my name off the credits.

▷ Merck refused to accept this and admonished me roundly. He declined to remove credits, or even give any credence to my resignation. "Say what you fucking like," he said, "but I don't accept it." "Please repair," said Rob. "Make a deal," said an inner voice. The new green version, on this page, was artistically superior, Merck claimed, from his lofty managerial position, and more suitable for the band, which was at least something he knew better about.

▷ This little saga was resolved in the end by Merck agreeing not to enforce design decisions in the future, since it was by and large not necessary (decisions being reached mutually). For our part we surrendered to his request and changed the design, as you can see, to the best of our abilities.

▷ Now, I can well imagine that this is not the most gripping story you've ever read, but it is central to a design ethic which believes in long term relations. The relationship itself is more important than any one specific item, and in this instance both sides had worked hard to maintain it. Yet again there are only so many items which make up a relationship. This one with Catherine Wheel will probably not survive another schism. Fidelity is one thing: uncritical devotion quite another. My dog told me that.

opposite: THUNDER "Like A Satellite" poster [1993]

THUNDER // LIKE A SATELLITE

One of the great pleasures of being a maker of pictures is that the results are there long after the original event to remind you of what you did and what you intended. This is, of course, particularly satisfying if you like the image. It doesn't matter that much to the person responsible whether he is Picasso, a Sunday painter or a graphic designer – the sense of achievement is still very strong. But there is a catch – if the image or picture is a failure then the after glow is severely diminished. If a design is disappointing then the designer can rarely look at it and is inclined to keep it under wraps, not thinking about it too often, or mentioning it out loud. The photographic studies on this and the previous page fall somewhere in between, for they certainly give pleasure, but they also perplex. I find them eerie and mildly erotic, yet I find the ambiguity disturbing, despite having generated it in the first place. The image seems to suggest violation without it actually occurring. The shadow is on her body, but the hand is not. How can a shadow be violent? It might threaten, like the long shadows in Film Noir, or the spidery hands and bony face of Nosferatu, but here it is just the shadow of a normal hand which we see cast upon her body. It's nothing real, just a shadow. What disturbs me is that I might want to suggest violation at all, that I might want to show a nude woman under threat, even if only shadowy, or in her mind. Dark forces here: shades of sexism perhaps: traces of misogyny. Makes me shudder, like she might if she knew the black shadow hand was reaching across her breast (unless she's masochistic, which is more disturbing). Yet I still appreciate the graphic qualities, and the seen but unseen nature of her flesh, more seductive, as pundits always maintain, when you can't see too much. Suggestion is all.

▷ The photography was simplicity itself, executed in a studio using tungsten lights, one of which was more focused (spotted) with the hand held in front throwing a shadow upon the elegant contours of our favourite model, the very lovely Kimberly Cowell (she graced *Shine On* for Pink Floyd and *Adam And Eve* and *Chrome* for Catherine Wheel). A real professional, as they say in the trade, often cheerful and never whingeing. There is no retouching here – what you see is what we saw – except we used tungsten film to warm the flesh tones.

▷ The client was Thunder, a hard rock, blues based outfit of modest stature, who earnt an honest crust plying their trade up and down the country. Still do by all accounts. This was a single bag for a song called 'Like A Satellite', but my memory fails to reveal the connection of the music to the design. Or does it? A hand reaching out to make contact, casting its shadow from afar, long distance communication, like a satellite. I knew it must have been something tangible because this image is not from the infamous cupboard but is originally conceived. That I know, without a shadow of a doubt.

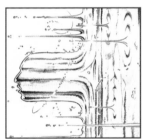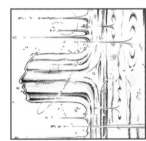

▷ The music is the starting point for all design ideas and we played it over and over again in varying circumstances. We read and re-read the lyrics. And we talked, scribbled, thought hard, and gradually accumulated snippets, doodles and phrases which evolved by further discussion and thinking into more concrete ideas and recognisable sketches. Two of the original rough ideas are shown here illustrated by Keith Breeden: one of an abstract chrome face emerging in streamlined style from a bed of liquid chrome, the other showing the tip and submerged part of a humanoid iceberg formation. Catherine Wheel said they

This is how we produced an album cover. The manager, Merck Mercuriadis, rang us up and asked if we'd be interested in designing an album cover for a band called Catherine Wheel. The manager was an ardent Pink Floyd fan and, although Catherine Wheel music was very different, he felt that they were (potentially) as important and relevant in the Nineties as Floyd had been in the Sixties. It is a manager's job to believe strongly in his band. Singer and songwriter Rob Dickinson, along with said manager, gave us a (brief) description of how they saw their music, and what the cover design might represent. I remember that they felt there was more to the music than might initially be thought. 'Tip of the iceberg' was a phrase that recurred. We were given a tape of some of the new material, as yet unfinished, plus all the lyrics to date, incomplete but annotated, and the previous album.

preferred this one, but would like it to be green because green was cool, and I'd done too many blue album covers; I agreed. (My son Bill's satiric appraisal of my work was "too many fields, horizon lines and blue skies". He said that I should call the book 'Blue Horizons', and walked away chuckling. Very funny.)

▷ First thing was to take a test in the shallow end of a local swimming pool, using an underwater 35 mm camera held at water level. The eyeline would be the surface of the water, like many a split level photo in *National Geographic* adorning articles about pond life or Amazonian toads. Despite the unattractive aquatic form of yours truly (don't laugh), yet owing much to the elegant shapes made by Chloe Mason (daughter of Floyd drummer Nick Mason), the idea looked promising. We found a location in Central London (the university student union swimming pool in Malet Street), hired some powerful tungsten lights, and

518 039-1

(LC) 0211   PG 281

fontana

Side One
KILL RHYTHM
I CONFESS
CRANK
BROKEN HEAD
PAIN
STRANGE FRUIT

Side Two
CHROME
THE NUDE
URSA MAJOR SPACE STATION
FRIPP
HALF LIFE
SHOW ME MARY

Produced by Gil Norton

devised a cunning method for taking the actual photographs. The underwater camera was dispensed with because of lack of quality/definition incurred by the intervening glass of the casing. We could not shoot through a porthole below the surface (though the location had one), because it was just that bit too far beneath the surface, so we used an ordinary rectangular fish tank held near the edge of the pool and submerged three quarters in the water, forming an air pocket, or rather a glass window/porthole of our own, now at water level. A junior bathysphere. By lying on the poolside our photographer Tony May could lean over and down into the fish tank with his trusty Hasselblad and take pictures like normal, except for a contorted position creating a certain discomfort, and plenty of complaint. ◁

The second major problem was the fitness of the models. Since the design of the human iceberg/pyramid involved being underwater for long periods it would require strong, aqua friendly lung masters, like…members of the university swimming club, or life guards with life saving certificates and shoulders like trees. Money changed hands and they duly obliged, but unfortunately with indifferent results. Tony lit the underwater formation by blasting a huge quantity of light from the side of the pool, slanted like artificial sun rays down at an angle into the water. He also used a little fill from the opposite side. But it was not enough. The water of the swimming pool absorbed more light than anticipated, and although the life guards performed feats of endurance while submerged they could not, bless them, adopt the elegant shapes we had in mind. This shoot was therefore labelled the 'second test', and we did it all again. ◁

The test had shown us that the idea at least worked, and that the junior bathysphere was functioning well. Most important, the split water level looked fantastic. But we still needed elegant shape makers; we needed dancers, dancers who could swim and hold their breath. Chloe Mason came to the rescue and set about recruiting personnel from the London Contemporary Dance School. We had also learned from the second test that white, loose fitting clothing was needed to reflect the light, and to allow the figures to stand out as clear shapes against the dark water behind. Loose clothing was preferable as it would undulate in the water. It was also quite important that it did not become sodden and heavy, dragging our unfortunate dancers down to a premature and watery grave.

▷ We shot again, correctly exposing this time, and the results were totally brilliant. When leaning over into the fish tank we could see the formation adopted by the dancers, but had no idea of how the water level was being registered on film, and that is because it was so close as to be severely out of focus, and also because it was moving and hence invisible over a long time exposure (varying from 1/30 to one second). We had therefore to shoot numerous variations without exhausting the dancers. This was accomplished by having a reserve team of aquanauts, who were not ballet dancers but professional models, and who were naked for the most part (p88/89), alternating in rota – one team performing whilst the other team rested.

▷ Peter Curzon deployed various elements in different parts of different formats, accompanied by clear elegant type and a discreet but beautifully appropriate layout. I particularly like the back of the

CATHERINE WHEEL "Chrome" [1993]
above: CD booklet
opposite: vinyl back

liked best, and also because different compositions suit the different proportions of the different formats. The front cover of this book is the CD cover, that on p85 is the cassette, and that on p86 is the vinyl…well, the back of the vinyl.

◗ Chrome is unashamedly a favourite of ours. A good and appropriate idea realised through resolute endeavour, cooperative teamwork and a slice of luck. The disembodied hand (see front of book) is actually the outstretched hand of the male dancer briefly visible above the water line. This is the tip of the iceberg, the tip

of the three dancers, who are floating below the water level. The soft wipe between above and below, between bronze hand and blue bodies, is created naturally by the moving water level, the gently lapping waves, passing up and down across the lens and across the field of vision. This photograph is a superimposition, a double image in different parts of the one frame, elegantly vignetted by chance and NOT assembled in the computer. There is no retouching here, no cleaning, no nothing. It's all done in the camera.

CATHERINE WHEEL "Chrome" CD booklet [1993]

vinyl (p84) – the dancer is leaping across the void and over the track list – and the back of the CD booklet (p87). We were able to persuade Catherine Wheel that their green bias cum blue prejudice should be forsaken because the actual blue was stupendous, deep and vivid, so intense that it required special five colour printing (standard four colours plus an extra blue) when released. We also suggested using different versions for different formats, partly because we couldn't decide which specific photo we

◗ In addition the vivid blue was astounding, better than reality, and completely unexpected, until the second test that is. It is caused, I think, by the gradual fall off of light through the water beyond, stretching back to the other end of the swimming pool. It's the perfect Blue Yonder. The water between camera and subject, moreover, served as a filter or net, lending a lustrous quality to the white highlights.

◗ In retrospect I continue to enjoy the elegance of the formation of bodies hanging mysteriously in the blue void, seemingly airborne yet not in air but underground, or underwater, representing visually that which is by definition not visible (one can only see the tip of an iceberg). An organic event for a metallic title (Chrome). An ethereal picture for a hard nosed band. A soft floating image for rock solid music.

The photograph opposite, for a single release by Thunder entitled 'A Better Man', involves a doomed love affair between a young woman from the land, and a young

A BETTER MAN

man from the sea. He is part man, part creature, covered naturally in kelp which sustains him, especially when he comes up for air. But time out of the sea is limited – he will soon have to return, and so forfeit the love they share. Their sadness is for a threatened happiness; they are resigned to the inevitability that land woman and sea man cannot survive, unmarked woman and patterned man are separated by habitat and by the nature of their skin. The seaweed is an encumbrance, not a painful

Some people get off on body disfigurement: they like to look at pictures of wounds, skin diseases, horrific burns, contusions and skin afflictions, or their equivalents custom made in the name of pleasure and torture. A hell of a lot more people get off on another kind of skin alteration, namely cosmetic decoration, ranging from ordinary western make-up to tribal ceremony, from theatre disguise to complex body painting. Alteration of the skin – changing what you look like, or might become – is clearly an extremely popular and deep seated preoccupation, bordering on the obsessional, vividly illustrating both our vanity and insecurity (and probably all psychological states in between). ◁

I am in neither of these camps. What holds fascination for me is the ambiguity, where the skin alteration is a mixture of the decorative and the afflicted, and where one is unsure if it's an illness or

VARIEGATED SKIN

executed on purpose, and where the effect is disquieting, hovering between seduction and repulsion. For example the illustration of the woman crouching on tip toe, poised possibly for action, like a warrior, shows her body covered in slugs, but unlike garden slugs these are nudibranches, or sea slugs, and are phenomenally beautiful, sporting bright colours and exotic patterns. The nudibranch woman is both stunning and ugly, attractive yet repellent. ◁

disfigurement, but still permanent and thus a barrier to their love. (That's real seaweed in case you're wondering.)
▷ The couple in the tiled bathroom are genetically pigmented like piebald horses. They are seen in private, for they are outcasts, and their pigmentation is not a disease but a disfigurement from birth, not physically uncomfortable, but culturally isolating. Piebald People, beautiful in their own way, but too weird to walk openly. In private they can be naked; they can be themselves. This design was produced from an excellent idea by Peter Christopherson and executed cleverly in the darkroom using acetate male/female masks, and appeared as a front vinyl cover for Kevin Godley and Lol Creme, whose album was called *Freeze Frame*.

▷ Last in our gallery of body-paint-skin-thingies is the profile head of a bald woman, long necked and defiant, not scared to walk abroad, no time for shame. She is proud, or aristocratic perhaps, and has developed small blood vessels on the outside of her skin, not inside like the rest of us. They cover her face, like the veins of a leaf, providing a variegated appearance, a mixture of the gruesome and the delicate, the vulnerable (easily punctured) and the confident (who will dare to puncture). At the same time it presents an incongruous reversal, where outside should be inside. She is inside out, or back to front, but seems not to notice. It's obviously all right with her. So perhaps it had better be all right with us.

THUNDER "A Better Man" single back [1993]

Sour grapes page, or the reasonable rant page, wherein distressed author sounds off (again) and rails against clients who, having turned him down, end up with crud. Rejection is especially bad for freelance folk like graphic designers because it's a double hit, bad for both the emotional and the financial balance. It's worse SCORPIONS news when the client then opts for indifferent alternatives, characterised by extreme moderateness, rather dull ideas and fairly ugly graphics. It seems to imply that your own offerings were actually inferior. When work is rejected it seems you don't get paid, you feel upset, AND you're told you're crap. When the emotional dust has settled and wounds have all but healed, it is time to question the underlying issues. If the saga is then repeated with the same client it becomes more questionable still. ◁

So come on in The Scorpions – lovable hard rock cum sentimental anthem cum sexist guitar heavy outfit from Hanover. Nice bunch of lads. Been grafting 25 years now. Durable at the least. Impeccable English, courteous and friendly, BUT oh so visually conservative at heart. We at Hipgnosis designed a cover for them back in the good ol' Seventies, called *Love Drive*, which they always thought was great (personally I have my doubts appearing, as it does, to reveal further layers of chauvinism). They came back years later for an album called *Pure Instinct* (1995) – one of the ideas was the couple copulating at the bottom of the stairs, their bodies seen in cut away section revealing their inner fantasies, which was to be produced photographically using the modern computer to great effect. Scientific sex. They turned it down, it later transpired, in favour of a humongous pile of crap in my opinion. (Courtesy and legality forbids showing it here.) ◁

Then in 1998 they commissioned me again for an album called *Eye To Eye*. I was of course reluctant to invite further humiliation, but I liked them, and thought it couldn't happen again. It just couldn't. But it did. Can you believe it? One of the rejected ideas is on the opposite page. At the time of writing I haven't yet seen what they preferred, but I'll wager that it's worse. This is not because of some overbearing sense of my own skill and talent (says who?), but much more because of their history of bad taste. They keep having dull covers. Paul McCartney was the same, and I should know because some of his dull covers came from

Hipgnosis, my old studio. (Shame on me, but I'm more mature now.) Many other rock bands do the same, like Oasis, Genesis or REM. Poor design comes obviously from poor designers, but also and as often it derives from poor clients. Clients who just don't think about it clearly, don't provide a correct or adequate brief, leave themselves too little time to make improvements or secure alternatives, or don't listen to advice or counsel, preferring instead to rely on their precious intuition or proclaimed authenticity. Don't hire a dog and bark yourself, I snarl.

▷ Having lousy covers is not that serious, of course, in the grand scheme of things, but in terms of making albums it's pretty central. So why have shit ones when one is aware that there are numerous good designers out there hungry for work, some of whom are known personally? Shooting yourself in the foot, is what it is. Or

stinging yourself to death, like mating scorpions. My theory is that it's all about safety. Bands are usually brave and experimental when they start out, when there is nothing to lose. Once established the shutters come down. Conservatism creeps in. Paul McCartney is conservative. The Scorpions are conservative, Mike Oldfield is conservative and so, for example, are Kiss, who also hired and fired me sometime during the late Eighties, not surprisingly. Kiss are, in my opinion, formulaic not innovative: more passionate about business than music; concerned not so much with the general human condition as with their private banking condition. Likewise Paul McCartney who is conservative from his head to his toes, and The Scorpions who are particularly conservative in terms of their perceived image, and hence their photos, videos and album covers. And all this conservatism despite protestations to the contrary, and in direct contrast to all that earlier postural guff when they were younger about

outrageous behaviour, freedom, sex and drugs, rebellion and attitude. Kiss and The Scorpions are outrageous to order, processed non conformity, black leather conservatism. Unadventurous music, unadventurous album covers.

SCORPIONS "Pure Instinct" rough [1995]

Eye II Eye

This image was conceived by me and Peter for a single release by the band Catherine Wheel called 'Judy Staring At The Sun'. Scary title: sounds as if she is immune in some way to the glare of the great orb. Has she lost all retinal sensation? Or is she in a trance, or out of her mind? Doesn't feel the heat, or perhaps her nerve ends are too frayed and she doesn't register pain! She'll go blind. In the song it seems all right for her to stare at the sun, too far gone to notice.

▷ She is more likely a heroin addict, cocooned in an opiate world, where pain is banished, where detachment reigns, and all is cool. So here, in our picture, she is entombed in a block of ice, which protects her from the outside world, and keeps her safe and secure. She sees the world, but only through her addiction, only through the layers of ice. So cool, so protected, and so trapped. She can stare at the sun all she wants, shielded from the heat of the glare by a translucent cold cage. She's calm now in her clear opiate box – her block of cool heroin ice.

▷ Tony May and I photographed this image in a small studio in Clerkenwell, London, using a Hasselblad and normal 80mm lens. The block of ice was placed on a 'canvas' backdrop, providing an old painterly texture, and then lit with tungsten light, picking out a few shiny reflective edges to accentuate the ice quality. The model – the slim, elegant and long suffering Tizer – took her pose under the same lighting conditions. CATHERINE WHEEL *JUDY STARING AT THE SUN*

▷ The two images were then combined seamlessly in the computer – an ordinary Mac in this case – by Richard Manning, with his endearing mixture of artistry and complaint. A particularly neat touch was to apply a ripple effect to the body (to look as though it were seen through the ice), but not all over (the ice might have clear patches). He also added some striations to the surface of the front face of the block to lend it further solidity.

▷ I provide these details for legal reasons, so that readers do not try this ice experiment at home with a younger sibling. Of course Tizer the model was actually entombed in two blocks of real ice slapped together temporarily, and rescued in the nick of time like Houdini, before she froze to death. But then she is a professional.

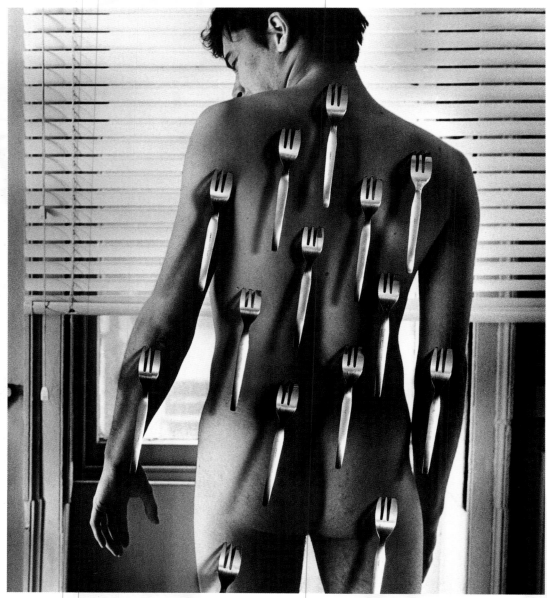

A penny for your fawkes

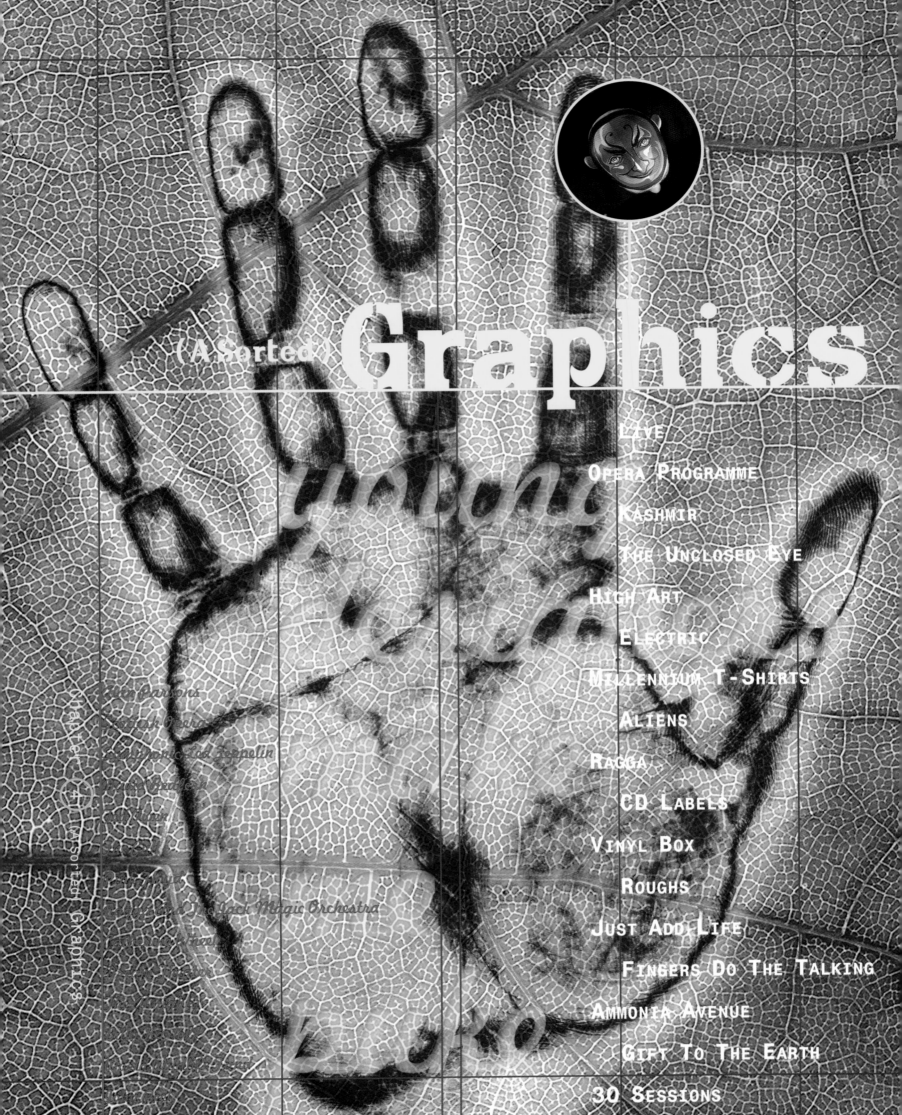

(A Sorted) **Graphics**

This section of our book, assorted graphics, is not only a mixed bag of graphic orientated designs which do not fit comfortably into other chapters, but it also forms a bridge between the more photographic (real) elements in the work and the more graphic (abstract) aspects. For example the cover for Billy Karloff (p137) is a photograph of something very graphic, namely a check tie, check shirt and check jacket (check it out). Alternatively there is 'Ragga' (p122) which is a photograph whose principal ingredients are illustrative. Then there are the photographic designs on this page, which are much more graphic than photographic, depending on shape and colour for effect rather than on narrative or setting. No huge production here, no complex photography, no deeper meanings. ◁

In fact nothing could be simpler, just some deep red liquid droplets on a light box, photographed in a little studio in Clerkenwell with a Nikon F using ordinary Ektachrome transparency and lit, if memory serves, with a single flash and a reflector. The liquid is red ink, or glycerine, and the shapes, at least on this page, are made partially by luck and partially with the aid of a blunt instrument (such as a pencil). The light box was used to provide muted underlight and a sense of translucency, and the normal off-white colour appeared blue because of underexposure. ◁

On the other hand, the droplets opposite are arranged more purposefully and they follow an Alan Parsons logo designed by Jon Crossland. The liquid is clearly three dimensional resting on the light box but is 'shaped' according to this AP logo. A computer retouching system was used to clean it up, deepen colour, and to move some droplets around to achieve the best composition.

▷ The droplets were given shiny highlights to accentuate their curvature. Jon's logo shape always looked to me like a graphic representation of a mother holding a baby, with an elongated right arm, and her head bent over towards the baby's head. It seemed like a universal symbol for motherhood and infant care. And when one turns the design 90 degrees, putting it on its feet, so to speak, the logo AP can be made out easily.

▷ And this is where the trouble started. A large part of the

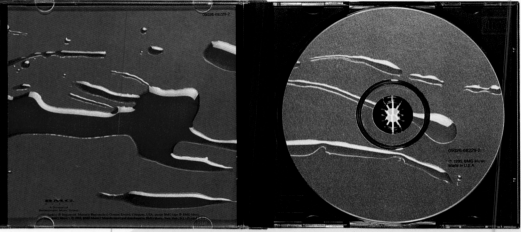

ALAN PARSONS LIVE

graphic attraction was this hidden AP. Mother and child and Alan Parsons – the mother of this album. The record company said they thought it neat, but wanted to permanently turn the design 90 degrees so the AP read normally, ie upright, not on its side, which is how it was initially designed, and from where the mother and baby was most apparent. Lo and behold, it came to pass that this would spoil the design, and the great American record company decided to go ahead anyway, change the cover and affix lettering to the front without consultation, without telling either me or Alan Parsons, until it was a fait accompli. Whoa there record company. You can't do that. You don't own the copyright and cannot reproduce it in a form other than specified. I huffed and I puffed and I threatened to withdraw my artwork. As I remarked to Alan, he wouldn't allow his music, his art, to be altered drastically without consultation and nor would I. I said jokingly that I could be bribed, or compensated, little believing that anyone would make me an offer. But lo and behold it came to pass that the record company did, through Alan's manager. (Or someone did.) Boy was I surprised. I asked for 10K dollars but got 6K. Six extra K for a bunch of droplets on a home made light box photographed in a small studio in half a day. It just goes to show the power of graphics, the subject of this particular chapter.

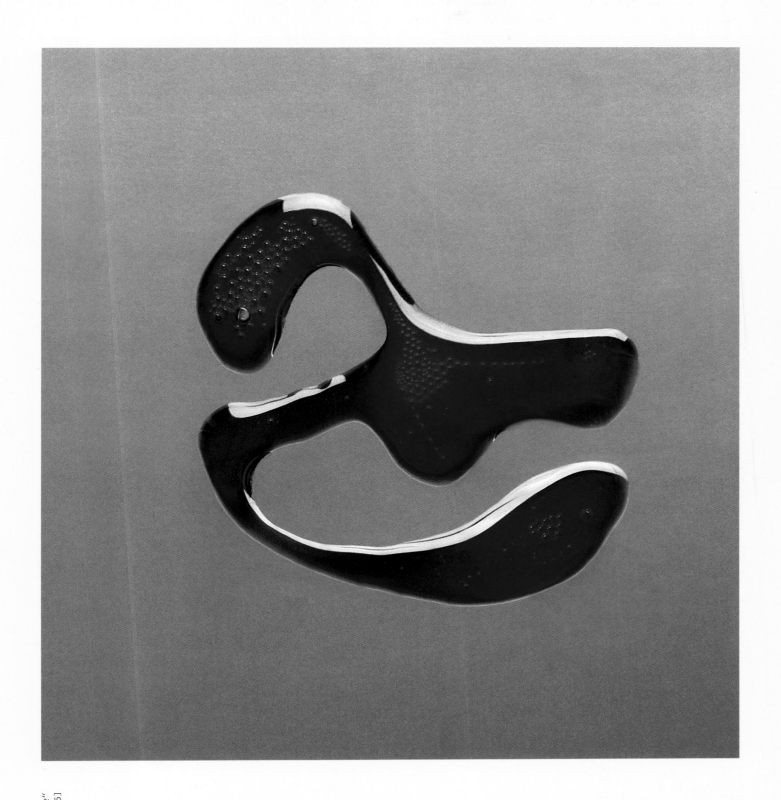

If one were to enumerate the principal attributes of opera they might include visions of heaving bosoms, flamboyant gestures, melodramatic situations, cascading music and full throttle singing. Whatever aficionados might say to the contrary, the characteristics that proclaim opera are the extravagant ones, and this is most definitely what I found when working on the season's brochure for Scottish Opera in 1998.

"I don't know much about opera," I protested on being asked if I'd be interested in the job. "That doesn't matter," replied Scottish Opera, in their charming and persuasive manner. "Many of our audience are not opera buffs and many of those we wish to attract are new, or relatively new, to opera. We hope to produce an innovative brochure to reflect the innovative approach of Scottish Opera," they added, "and it is breaking new ground to get a rock designer to do it. Do you think you can illustrate a diverse set of operas for our brochure? That's the question." (And on a limited budget, not because they're Glaswegian but because they are supported by the Arts Council and don't have a load of money.) We agreed from the outset that if most opera, including many of those for their upcoming season, was characterised by a full bloodedness, by an emotional tidal wave of music and singing, then the brochure should be equally full blooded. It should be richly illustrated, every page a full bled photo or design, and to cap it all, every background upon which text would appear would also be fully illustrated and fully bled. Pictures to the edge, to their fullest extent, like opera itself.

▷ I immersed myself in eight operas. I played opera music non stop for three weeks. I read the programme notes, I read the summaries, I read articles about the operas and their composers. It was a crash course. I tried my very best, but it was truly all too much. The inside of my head was an operatic Clapham Junction, like the photograph on p180/181 depicting a snake mating festival, as Puccini got entangled with Verdi, Mozart jostled with both Delius and Janacek: new operas (*Castro*) got mixed up with old ones (*Aida*), light stuff (*Magic Flute*) with heavy stuff (*Tristan And Isolde*), and tragedy (*La Bohème*) with fairy tale (*Hansel And Gretel*). Stories of betrayal, superstition and murder became entwined with those of sadness, infidelity and heartbreak. Princes and princesses rubbed shoulders in my operatic ferment with artisans and woodcutters, courtesans and military leaders. And loads of powerful music and lots of soaring vocals, much like the windswept clouds and heavy seas of the inset illustration overleaf.

▷ But I knew no better than to approach matters in the same way as I did rock music. So we sat around my studio and listened to the music, and thought about it, and listened some more, and scribbled copious notes and doodles until themes and images began to emerge. Ideas concretised into rough sketches, which were then submitted to Scottish Opera. They liked most of them and bid us get on with the photography in all haste. Opposite is the programme front cover, the spiral staircase, which was in fact shot at the end after all the inside pictures were taken. This image already contains a musical type shape (the spiral),

SCOTTISH OPERA season brochure [1998]

overleaf: "La Bohème"

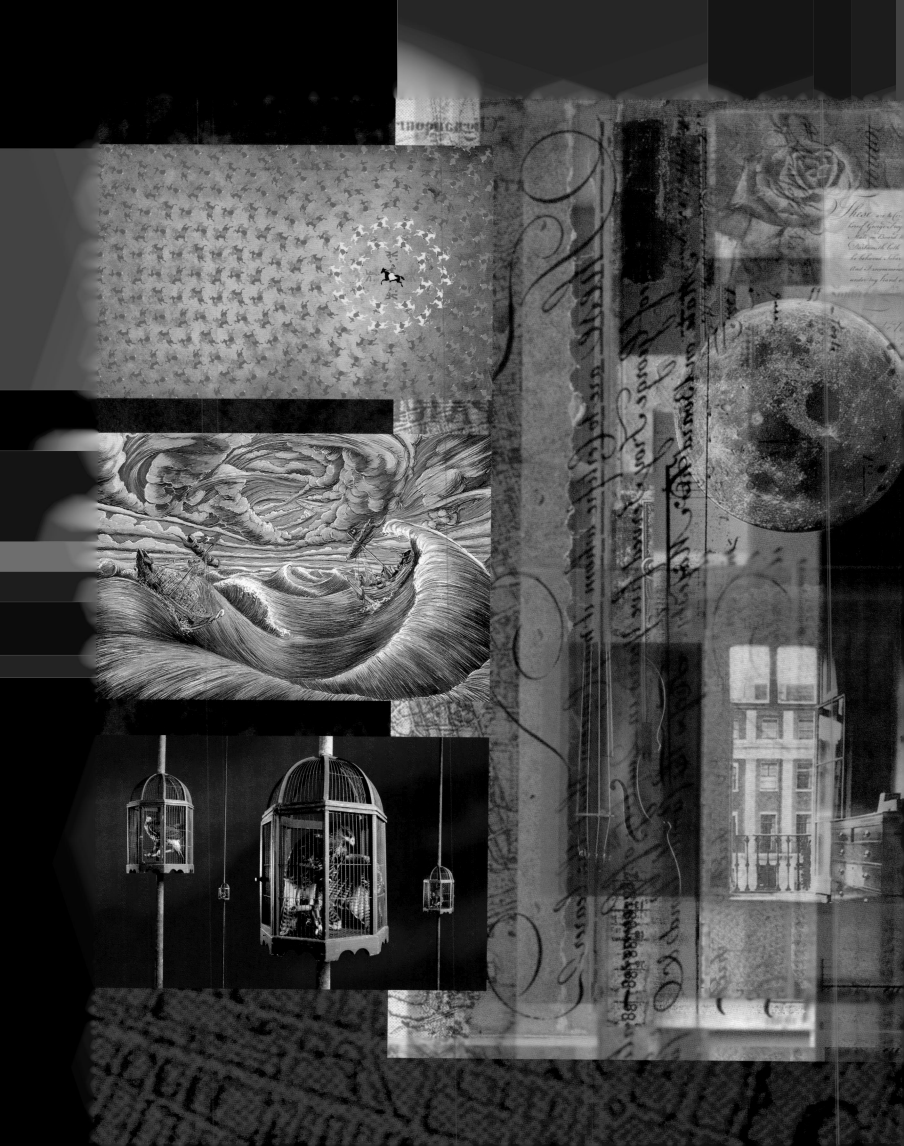

which in turn felt like an echo, a long (vocal) note falling away to the bottom of the stairs, at the same time suggesting a story without being too explicit, not favouring any one opera over another, since this was the front cover for a season of diverse operas. The figures could represent the two fundamental ingredients of opera – music and words (birdcage and books) – and resonate with the dramatic illustration (on p102) of two boats heading towards each other, the 'song boat' and the 'word boat', tossed about on the rolling waves of music. The flags fluttering from the mast are red and green, like the shirts worn by the figures on the spiral stairs, and like the red and green of the corrugated dust jacket seen on p100. ◁

The bottom inset picture (p102) is a graphic illustration designed by Peter for *Inez de Castro*, a modern opera dealing with perennial themes of betrayal and murder, though particularly concerned with an isolated figure in a foreign court, surrounded by potential enemies, a stranger in their own but adopted house. The eagle in the cage is illustrating the Czech opera *Dalibor*, which is a very melodramatic story of a national hero wrongfully imprisoned. (The repeated cages motif was stolen from Terry Gilliam's *The Time Bandits* but don't tell him.) The background collage spreading across p102/103 was intended to represent *La Bohème* and comprised numerous elements from the story (hand, candle, buttons, moon etc), set against pieces of handwritten manuscript encircling the doomed lovers. The whole illustration was put together artfully, since the male protagonists in the story are artists, and in a modest style as befits the bohemian setting

(despite being technically rendered on the Mac computer by Jon Crossland!).

▷ Scottish Opera said they were delighted with their brochure and that, no matter my misgivings, the whole exercise had worked really well. (They'd had lots of positive feedback and even some press coverage on the programme design itself.) Of course I was pleased by any praise, but in my heart I felt critical. I have only included the brochure illustrations that are okay…another 50% were regretfully not fit to be displayed. This critique is not false modesty. Sometimes ideas are not strong enough, the design is weak and the photograph is poorly produced. We had no time to edit back then, but I do now, in this book. I told Scottish Opera of my doubts, which they dismissed eloquently, but no repair was undertaken, no replacements or amendments were made to subsequent but related advertising material. I was guilty of biting off more than I could chew, being greedy and overblown, like some parts of many of the operas I was trying to visually represent. This was a great shame for a design mentality rooted in rock music because opera was refreshing and challenging, and made an interesting change. And we all know that a change is as good as a rest.

▷ The back cover of the brochure on this page tried to extend the spiral staircase story from the front, and consisted of open books flapping or gliding like birds in flight down to the bottom of the staircase, constituting, if you will, the results of the collision between the two figures approaching each other on the spiral stair at the top. The music is what makes the words (books) fly and become singing birds.

opposite (inset pic):
SYMPHONIC LED ZEPPELIN "Kashmir" CD front [1997]

ALAN PARSONS "Brother Up In Heaven" CD single [1996]

chapter two {**the sixties**}

chapter three {**the seventies**}

Diplomacy is not, I hasten to inform, one of my better points, otherwise I would not be speaking so freely of a book project produced by our own publisher, Sanctuary, and whose author therefore is in the same stable. Too close for comfort, too risky for truth. Peter and I designed a book of music photographs of the very charming David Redfern, who has been to more gigs than London Electricity. He has a roster to die for, especially of famous jazz musicians. Here are some chapter headings which Peter designed and the front cover image which neither David nor Sanctuary liked, but I did. The big hand – David's – holding a little camera suggested the sensitivity of both the photography and the man himself (the Hasselblad was his favourite camera). The shape of the fingers is eye like, as in the 'Unclosed Eye', and the repeated squares, or tabs, extend cleverly from the camera outline, arranged in rows like a modern computer keyboard, forming a layer on top like a veil to be drawn aside, and containing occasional inset photos of great and famous musicians. What more could Sanctuary want? Must've been something, because they turned it down in this form (which was already the second version), saying it was too busy. Too busy my arse! I hate being turned down, so I'm going to be real mature about it and simply put it in my book, in another of their own publications, just to spite them. Yeah.

chapter four {**the eighties**}

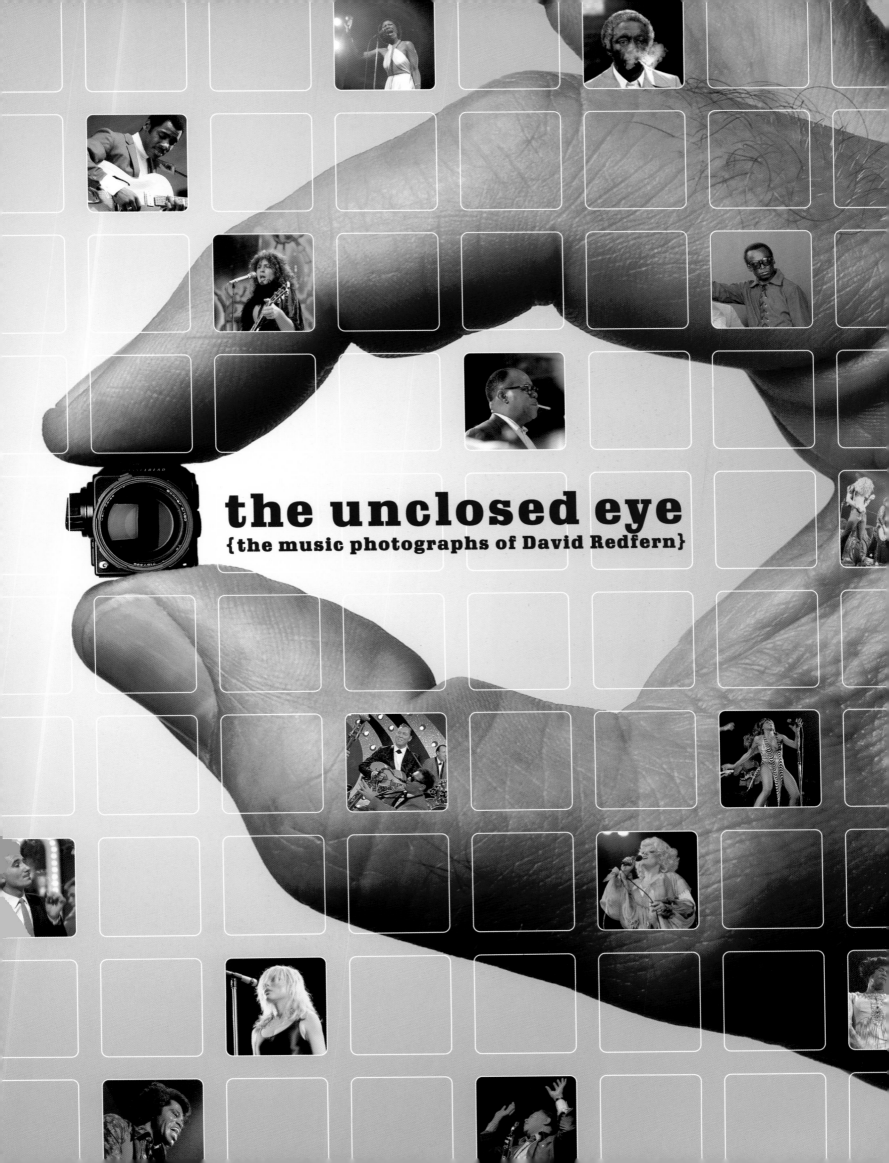

the unclosed eye
{the music photographs of David Redfern}

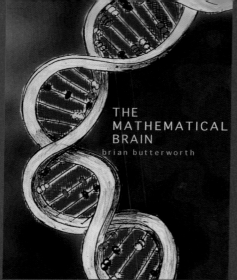

THE MATHEMATICAL BRAIN
brian butterworth

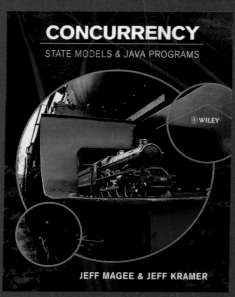

CONCURRENCY
STATE MODELS & JAVA PROGRAMS

WILEY

JEFF MAGEE & JEFF KRAMER

MIND OVER MATTER
THE IMAGES OF PINK FLOYD

THE BOOK OF TIME

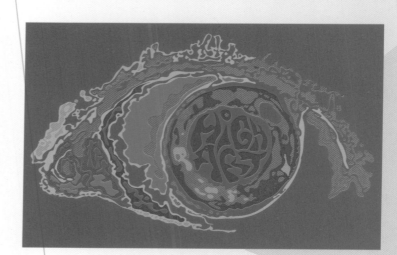

Book covers can be harder to design than album covers especially when the publisher is anxious about selling, which he usually is. These fatalistic covers, far left, include a rejected design for a popular science book on numbers, a published design for a computer text book, our own previous opus *Mind Over Matter* (which you should of course also get), and the cover for a proposed book whose time has not yet come.

High Art is a book by Ted Owen about psychedelic posters and contains obviously some fab art from the Sixties but also two innovative design features, or so I believe, namely changing type columns, and secondly blushed pages providing a muted but psychedelic background to text in fitting contrast to normal white. I doff my hat to the high art but low scruples of my colleagues Jon Crossland and John McGill.

THE CULT * ELECTRIC

I met Keith Breeden through Malcolm Garrett, himself a fine designer, and I would not have guessed how well we would get on. Keith was plain speaking, rather gruff and anti intellectual, keen on motorbikes, and came from Manchester (along with Malcolm and another famous cover designer, Peter Saville). He was an excellent illustrator, a fine graphic designer (Scritti Politti, Fine Young Cannibals, ABC, The Mission) but he hated the music business, especially petty minded record company personnel and complex money hassles, unappreciative musicians and cheating managers. He was committed equally to doing his best and to speaking his mind. We collaborated on Ellis Beggs & Howard, Thunder, Pink Floyd and The Cult, who wanted a cover after the style of Rick Griffin (*Aoxomoxoa* for The Grateful Dead) which was always a mystery to me. Why should they want that? They claimed it (ie Griffin type design) was very rock 'n' roll, but I never understood what they were getting at. Keith designed and drew a Griffin type Cult logo and deployed it for an album and two singles in slightly different ways as shown. In retrospect I suppose it was insulting. It was certainly ill advised. They should have had a 'Keith Breeden' not a 'Rick Griffin' – more suitable, more authentic, more honest. The work is okay but who wants to copy somebody else? I like to think we did the job so we could work together rather than for The Cult. And where are they now I'd like to know? I know where Keith is. He left the design business and decamped to rural Wales and a very different life altogether – rolling hills, a lovely wife, and three young children. Perhaps he's a lucky man.

Nick Mason, drummer of Pink Floyd, is sometimes described as one of the funniest and one of the luckiest men in rock 'n' roll, and was enthusiastic in his own sporadic way about these Pink Floyd Millennium T-shirts, whereas David Gilmour, lead guitar, vocals and current Floyd torch bearer, had a somewhat muted reaction. More than eight months of intermittent and delicate negotiations finally secured agreement on the Millennium T-shirt range. I always wanted to design a range of fashion accessories since my fashion sense is openly derided by my colleagues, and my children (and by the Floyd). The merchandising company also delayed matters, reluctantly and belatedly agreeing to my design requests that the T-shirts would have old Pink Floyd cover PINK FLOYD/MILLENNIUM T-SHIRTS designs on the back, and brand new designs on the front, and not vice versa. I won this battle by lying through my teeth, abusing the Floyd position I'm in, and old-fashioned blackmail. ("If you don't do it this way the band won't let you do it at all!") I had tried diplomacy and rational argument but they hadn't worked. The new designs were of primary concern, naturally, and I listened again to the albums and re-read all the lyrics. In effect I repeated the procedure that had produced the cover designs in the first place (*Dark Side*, *WYWH* etc) to produce these current ideas. The designs needed to be more graphic than photographic, because this works better in terms of clothing material and the process of printing on fabrics. ◀

we wanted new designs mostly
not old ones
nor reworked ones
so we
listened again to the albums
and re-designed from scratch
from the music and
from themes in the lyrics
observant floydians will detect
history's serpentine head whilst
dedicated followers of fashion
can enjoy the novel armpits
and sentimentalists can wear
the items back to front
we aim to please

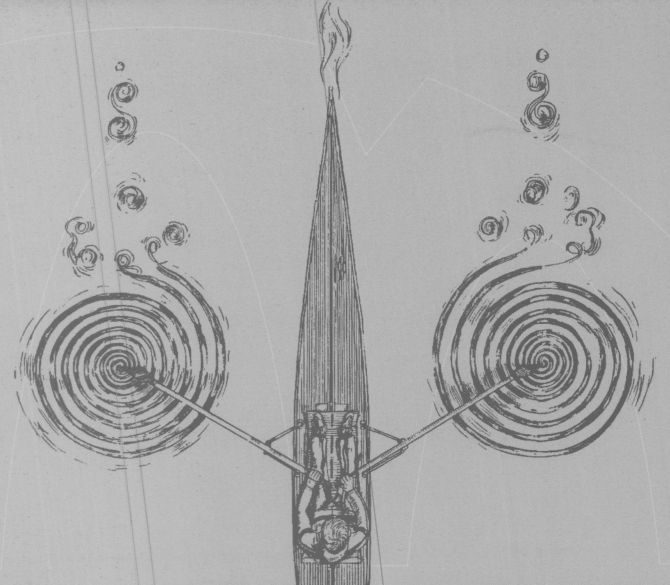

Dark Side (p117) contains a constellation of the three main themes of the album (madness, lost opportunity and megalomania), arranged and connected graphically by suitable prism like triangular shapes: a shape which appropriately determined the end of the range shirt (see previous page), where a big triangle or prism is subdivided by various smaller triangles containing sections of all the relevant Floyd covers. Very elegant, very fitting. I also enjoy the new front to *Ummagumma* – instead of a cover within a cover, we have a T-shirt within a T-shirt ad infinitum. I'll leave you Floyd fans to decode *Momentary Lapse*, and the story behind *Animals*. For those of you who are not Floyd fans…why aren't you? Haven't you been taking the tablets I gave you?

PS The Alan Parsons T-shirt has crept in here in deference to Mr Nick Stone of Muswell Hill N10, who drew the illustration and is responsible for helping to organise much of this book. (Got to keep him on my side.) The picture contains visual clues to all Alan's albums, and the viewer's job is to locate and name them. Fun if you're a fan. If you're not…why aren't you? Haven't you been taking…

ALAN
PARSONS
LIVE
PROJECT

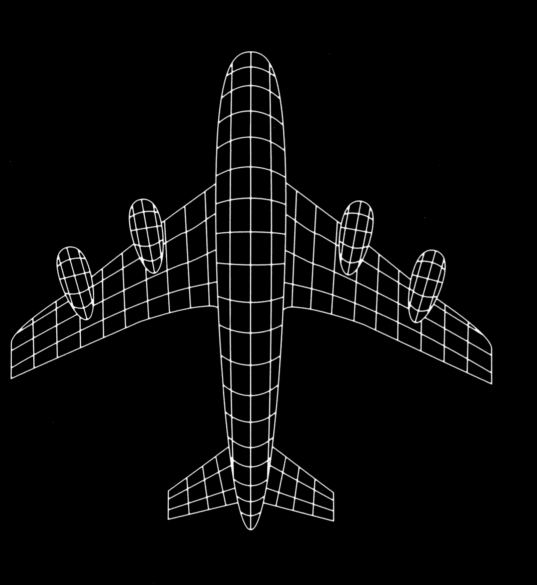
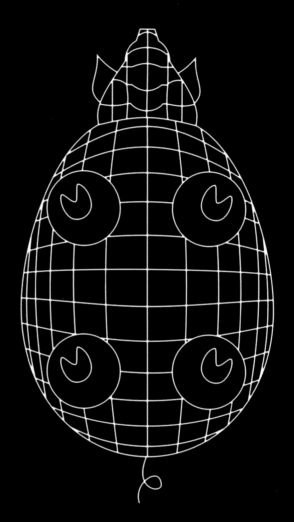

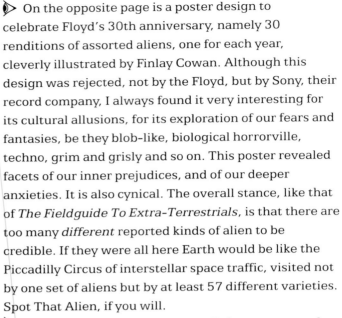

I've had it up to here with aliens. Half the world thinks they're already here, conspiring with the government, or holed up under the ice, hiding behind the planet Jupiter or occupying a 'time ripple', wherein they have always been here on Earth, so this thesis goes, but existing in a different time frame. By accident, or by design, they slip, via a time ripple, into our time reference, and so appear randomly, only to disappear again just as mysteriously back into their own time frame. This, you'll appreciate, is a neat argument in favour of UFOs and accounts for their sporadic appearances, here and gone…otherwise one might ask where are all the UFOs parked when not appearing to exhausted pilots or oddballs in Nevada. This 'time ripple' thesis also neatly sidesteps the problem of interstellar travel: it's no longer a question of how aliens ever got here across the vast reaches of space, because they already are here, but in a different time zone. It's not that I don't believe in UFOs and aliens, but rather that I'll think about it more seriously when they arrive at the UN or outside the Kremlin. To believe is to relegate aliens to religion, which is not, I'm inclined to think, what UFO-ologists desire. ◁

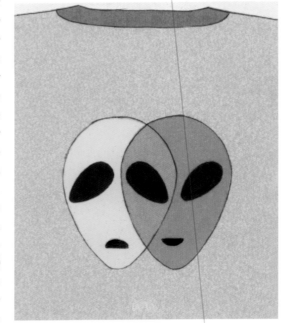

However, the subject of aliens is very interesting for the other issues which it raises, such as the origins of life, the psychology of belief, some fundamental aspects of religion, of engineering and of technology, and many problems of astronomy and cosmology. For the more 'lofty' purpose of design, however, I have used aliens for Pink Floyd, who else? They feature in the range of Millennium T-shirts, specifically *Saucerful Of Secrets* (shown here). I reworked the comedy/tragedy masks from theatre-land and overlapped a depressed alien (standard 'grey' model) with a happy alien, such that they neatly, so I thought, shared the same middle 'eye'. Not only was this intended to reflect songs on the album ('Heart Of The Sun', 'Let There Be Light'), but it also referred to the departure of Syd Barrett and the arrival of David Gilmour.

▷ On the opposite page is a poster design to celebrate Floyd's 30th anniversary, namely 30 renditions of assorted aliens, one for each year, cleverly illustrated by Finlay Cowan. Although this design was rejected, not by the Floyd, but by Sony, their record company, I always found it very interesting for its cultural allusions, for its exploration of our fears and fantasies, be they blob-like, biological horrorville, techno, grim and grisly and so on. This poster revealed facets of our inner prejudices, and of our deeper anxieties. It is also cynical. The overall stance, like that of *The Fieldguide To Extra-Terrestrials*, is that there are too many *different* reported kinds of alien to be credible. If they were all here Earth would be like the Piccadilly Circus of interstellar space traffic, visited not by one set of aliens but by at least 57 different varieties. Spot That Alien, if you will.

▷ The perceptive reader may well detect a tone of angry scepticism and he or she would be correct. This scepticism stems not only from my irreligious and rational disposition (generally speaking), but also from the direct experience, not of aliens, but of making a documentary for Discovery TV called *Are We Alone* about the existence of aliens. The experience for all concerned was awful: for Discovery because they hated my film, and for me because they changed my film after I left so I hated it. It was a labour of love, this documentary, and it upset me deeply that it backfired so badly. Discovery wanted, I suspect, alien vignettes à la Pink Floyd, whereas I wanted what I discovered via research, which was the likelihood that aliens did not exist, supported by the reasoning and issues which informed this conclusion. The absence of evidence is not evidence of absence, but it certainly constituted the beginning of what to me was a fascinating, intellectual journey. Then again what would television want with such a beast? If it results in the non-existence of aliens, it's not a ratings conscious item, not a sexy TV subject, as they call it in media-land. Just think how many hours of TV are spent, or wasted, on assessing the existence of something that doesn't exist. For your edification then, herewith is a condensed reworked version of the ill fated unseen TV documentary subtitled 'A Rational Argument Against Aliens':

THE ARGUMENT IN BRIEF

☻ ALIENS WILL BE SOMETHING LIKE US. IN ORDER TO COMMUNICATE SO THAT WE CAN KNOW THAT THERE ARE ALIENS HERE AT ALL, THEY WILL HAVE TO OCCUPY THE SAME UNIVERSE AS WE DO, EVEN TEMPORARILY, AND HENCE BE SUSCEPTIBLE TO THE SAME PROPERTIES AND LAWS AS WE ARE.

☻ ALIENS WILL BE SOMETHING LIKE US BECAUSE THE SAME ELEMENTS, THE SAME BUILDING BLOCKS AND THE SAME CHEMISTRY ARE FOUND EVERYWHERE IN OUR SOLAR SYSTEM, IN OUR GALAXY, AND IN OTHER GALAXIES. SCIENTISTS SEE THE SAME CHEMISTRY IN ALL DIRECTIONS IN SPACE. IT IS THE SAME STUFF AND THE SAME PROCESSES EVERYWHERE.

☻ ALIENS LIKE US WILL NEED CONDITIONS LIKE OURS (AN EARTH-SOMEWHERE-ELSE) TO EXIST. THESE CONDITIONS DO NOT OCCUR EVERYWHERE IN THE GALAXY, AS THEY DO NOT IN OUR OWN SOLAR SYSTEM. THERE MAY BE BILLIONS OF STARS OUT THERE BUT NOT BILLIONS OF PLANETS SUITABLE FOR LIFE.

☻ LIFE DOES NOT NECESSARILY OCCUR ON ALL THOSE PLANETS SUITABLE FOR LIFE. IF THE OCCURRENCE OF LIFE IS AN UNLIKELY EVENT, THEN THERE WILL BE VERY FEW ACTUAL LIFE BEARING PLANETS.

☻ INTELLIGENT 'HUMAN' LIFE, IE LIFE WITH TECHNOLOGY, IS VERY RARE ON EARTH (IE ONLY ONE SPECIES, MAN), SO WILL NOT ARISE OFTEN ON LIFE BEARING PLANETS ELSEWHERE, IF AT ALL. THERE MAY BE LOWLY ALIEN FORMS BUT NOT HIGHER FORMS, INTELLIGENT AND TECHNOLOGICAL ENOUGH TO CROSS INTERSTELLAR SPACE.

☻ THERE IS NO CLEAR CUT EVIDENCE OF ALIENS; NO SPECIMENS, NO HARDWARE, NO CORROBORATION, NO RADIO SIGNALS, ON EARTH, OR IN THE SUR-ROUNDING GALAXY. THE MOST LIKELY EXPLANATION FOR THIS DEARTH OF EVIDENCE IS THAT ALIENS DO NOT EXIST.

☻ FERMI'S 'PARADOX' ALLEGES THAT IF ALIENS DO EXIST THEN THEY SHOULD BE HERE, IF THEY ARE NOT HERE THEN THEY DO NOT EXIST. THIS ARGUMENT RESTS ON THE IDEA THAT IF ALIENS DID EXIST THEY WOULD BE FAR IN ADVANCE OF US TECHNOLOGICALLY (HAVING EMERGED BEFORE US) AND WOULD HAVE HAD PLENTY OF TIME TO GET HERE. SO WHERE ARE THEY?

☻ NONE OF THE EXPLANATIONS FOR WHY THERE ARE NO ALIENS IS VERY CONVINCING. THE MOST LIKELY ONE IS THAT THEY DON'T EXIST (OCCAM'S RAZOR).

☻ CLINCHER 1 – MANY EXPERTS ACTUALLY BELIEVE THAT THE EMERGENCE OF INTELLIGENCE HERE IS A FLUKE AND WOULD NOT HAPPEN AGAIN EVEN IF THERE WERE LOTS OF OTHER PLACES FOR IT TO DO SO. NO INTELLIGENCE, NO TECHNOLOGY, AND THEREFORE NO ALIENS.

☻ CLINCHER 2 – THE SPECIFIC CONDITIONS (DISTANCE FROM THE SUN, POLAR AXIS, PRESENCE OF MOON, ETC) THAT PROVIDE FOR OUR EARTH ARE SO COMPLEX AND FINELY TUNED, THAT THE CHANCE OF AN EARTH-SOMEWHERE-ELSE IS EXTREMELY LOW. THERE MAY NOT IN FACT BE AN EARTH-SOMEWHERE-ELSE. THEREFORE NO OTHER LIFE PLANETS. THEREFORE NO ALIENS.

By way of a postscript. At some point in the alien debate many people question the definition of life – perhaps it could be very different from our own and not need an Earth-somewhere-else. The argument goes like this. Look, the universe is a darn big place and we may discover it to be very different from what we think. It is sheer arrogance to assume if aliens exist then they'd be in a form detectable by us. How can you be so sure that aliens are not so exotic that they are unknowable, hence not detectable, and not open to rational speculation?

The apparent validity of this argument rests on the belief that radically different extra-terrestrial life cannot be shown to be true or false. For whilst it may be true that they are really bizarre aliens, it may also be false. If they are undetectable there is no way to decide, and many people see this impasse as grounds enough for sustaining a belief in intelligent alien life. But are they then willing to accept the implications of 'unknowable aliens', of beings comprised of something other than atoms, that change states without using energy, and have no effect on the material universe? Furthermore the apparent 50/50 balance (there are either bizarre aliens or there are not) is misleading. History demonstrates that in unverifiable arguments the rational position is more often carried, eg does the Sun revolve round the Earth (religious doctrine) or the Earth round the Sun (reasoned conclusion).

RAGGA & THE JACK MAGIC ORCHESTRA CD booklet back [1997]

Some bands think that working with me is a pain in the butt – can't imagine why – and probably feel that their album covers didn't do them much good anyway. I have to confess that working for some bands is not always wonderful and can very occasionally be truly awful. Sometimes it all gets too much, and Ragga was just one such occasion. ◁

Not the job itself, you understand, though that was difficult enough, what with finding several bald headed people, including one girl, upon whose heads to paint our 'faces', available at the one and same time, and what with our photographer having a bad day and underexposing, and then the record company EMI deciding at the last moment not to put the band on the front, but on a slip case fortunately (saving me a coronary). No, it wasn't the job but the effing band. Not all the band, just one of them. ◁ Ragga was an Icelandic couple plus one English guy. He was fine. She was great. But her husband was deeply insecure. Kept changing his mind; kept fussing over details, wanting to alter things, making things perfect, as he put it, but generating instead a profusion of intrusion. He questioned things, made us do alternatives, asked us to illustrate his own ideas, changed things back again, and wanted to discuss everything in what seemed like endless and interminable detail. And to cap it all he wanted to involve his manager, not at the outset but three quarters of the way down the line. Kiss of death or what? ◁

The central idea was about pictures in your head, like stories in the mind, like the songs on the album. The trompe l'oeil signified a different perspective, kind of odd and unexpected like the music. Faces looking up, and/or looking in front. The actual face, and the drawn face, are 'sharing' the real ears: and these different faces are what represented the individual tracks on the album. They were designed by Jon Crossland, Finlay Cowan and myself after lengthy discussions with Ragga, and were painted by Phyllis Cohen, and then photographed (from above) in a studio in North London, using tungsten lighting, a Hasselblad and normal transparency film. The idea was an extension of a TV commercial I had made for Pink Floyd where the same clown face was painted on several bald headed people. For Ragga we developed the idea by changing the faces so they were all different – some were human, or doll like, some were animals, and some others were not faces at all, but spiral staircases, or a trap door, or a cracked egg. These then appeared in the CD booklet.

The whole shebang was rounded off by Jon Crossland with some excellent starburst graphics, a sort of crazy fusion of cheap pop and Arabic wisdom. What more could they want?

▷ Well, there must have been something, because Mr Ragga Man continued to try and change things, whether it was the actual head illustrations or the lettering, the front cover crop, or the band's logo. Fortunately (as I see it) he was poorly, and missed the actual photoshoot, and then ran out of time during the artwork stage owing to release dates. The entire episode taxed me greatly – if it wasn't for the understanding and patience of the record company, particularly Tony Harlow, I'd have lost it for sure. Not knowing what to do next or which way to look, just like the figures in our picture on the opposite page.

Tails you win, heads I lose. (But I don't really because I've still got a design I like a lot, not only for the trompe l'oeil, or for the metaphor of pictures in the head, but also because you can view it any which way. The picture here is the same as the frontispiece (p5), but the other way up, and it doesn't look quite the same. One has difficulty seeing things upside down, or the wrong way round. Perhaps the Ragga baldheads don't since they can see in two directions at once.)

BRUCE DICKINSON "Skunkworks" CD label [1996]

© 1996 Redline Enterprises Ltd.

LC 6448

ANTHRAX *fueled*

© 1995 Elektra Entertainment Group, a division of Warner Communications Inc. for the United States and WEA International Inc. for the world outside of the United States. All Rights Reserved. A Time Warner Company. Unauthorized duplication is a violation of applicable laws. Made in U.S.A. by WEA Manufacturing Inc. Licensed for promotion only · Not for sale.
Prcd 9345-2

CATHERINE WHEEL
Ma Solituda (Edit) 4:09
COMPOSED BY **Catherine Wheel**

Chrysalis.
CDCHSDJ 5077
LC 1626

PRODUCED BY **GGGarth, Bob Ezrin** AND **Rob Dickinson**
ENGINEERED AND MIXED BY **Randy Staub**
For Promotional Purposes Only - Not For Resale.
℗ 1998 THE COPYRIGHT IN THIS SOUND RECORDING IS OWNED BY
Chrysalis Records Ltd. © 1998 **Chrysalis Records Ltd.** THIS LABEL.
COPY INFORMATION IS THE SUBJECT OF COPYRIGHT PROTECTION.
ALL RIGHTS RESERVED. © 1998 **Catherine Wheel** UNDER
EXCLUSIVE LICENCE TO **Chrysalis Records Ltd.**
MADE IN U.K.

THE CRANBERRIES

BURY THE HATCHET

WARNING: UNAUTHORIZED REPRODUCTION OF THIS RECORDING IS PROHIBITED BY FEDERAL LAW AND SUBJECT TO CRIMINAL PROSECUTION. MADE IN THE U.S.A. PRCD 6003-2 — ISLAND RECORDS, INC. A POLYGRAM COMPANY, 825 EIGHTH AVE., N.Y., NY 10019 ℗©1999 ISLAND RECORDS LTD. ALL RIGHTS RESERVED

10cc Mirror Mirror

DREAM THEATER
Burning My Soul

℗ 1997 ELEKTRA ENTERTAINMENT GROUP, A DIVISION OF WARNER COMMUNICATIONS INC. FOR THE UNITED STATES. A TIME WARNER COMPANY. ALL RIGHTS RESERVED. UNAUTHORIZED DUPLICATION IS A VIOLATION OF APPLICABLE LAWS. FOR PROMOTION ONLY—NOT FOR SALE PRCD 9998-2

ween

1. Mutilated Lips
(album version)
(WEEN; WARNER-TAMERLANE PUBLISHING/
VER MUSIC/BROWNDOG MUSIC, BMI)
PRODUCED BY ANDREW WEISS
℗ 1997 ELEKTRA ENTERTAINMENT GROUP, A DIVISION
OF WARNER COMMUNICATIONS INC. FOR THE UNITED
STATES AND WEA INTERNAOG MUSIC, BMI).

BRUCE DICKINSON
SKUNKWORKS

LIVE

1. Inertia
2. Faith
3. Innerspace
4. The Prisoner

CD2
1. Trial of Tears 2. Hollow Years 3. Take Away My Pain
4. Caught in a Web 5. Lie 6. Peruvian Skies 7. John
Petrucci guitar solo 8. Pull Me Under Medley:
9. Metropolis 10. Learning To Live
11. A Change of Seasons VII: The Crimson Sunset
Produced by Kevin Shirley

ONCE IN A LIVE TIME

DREAM THEATER

PINK FLOYD 30TH (1997)

albums would be included plus *Piper* because that was the one that was actually 30 years old.

▷ So seven vinyl albums in a robust box. A curious number I thought. More curious was their desire to keep all the packaging as it first was (for purity's sake), but not *Wish You Were Here*, because the original opaque plastic shrink wrap was too expensive to repeat: nor *Relics* because they wanted to promote the repackaged image not the original one: and not *Piper* because it wasn't a gatefold before but they wanted it to be so now like the others in the box. Curiouser and curiouser. And all seven album covers needed to be different from before, in some minor way, in order to distinguish them as remastered, not original. More curious still was that EMI managed to use entirely the wrong sound masters (digital instead of analogue), and had

What a muddle! One would think after many years in the business that both the group and the record company would know what they're doing. For some reason beyond my comprehension, EMI (Floyd's record company) decided to commemorate 30 years of Pink Floyd by releasing a vinyl box set. Perhaps it was all that the band would allow by way of celebration, disliking birthdays perhaps, or worried about their age? Or their inertia? Or too much cashing in? Either way the record company felt that six

to recall all the boxes anyway one month after going on sale to the public! Quel horreur! They blamed the manager, who denied everything. Surprise surprise.

▷ Despite all these anomalies and cock-ups we enjoyed the exercise by creating new but old stickers – out of focus circular renditions of original cover images – and attaching them to the old vinyl covers. As you can see, dear reader, this gives a reverse microscope type effect (p128), a sort of distorted worm's eye view, a binocular detail that is less clear, rather than more clear, than the complete thing. Defocused cows and prisms stared out of a central hole cut in the actual box, like an old 45, and informed you what was inside, but that it was different. Since the stickers were easily removable, purists and die hard fans could peel them off and reveal the originals. In addition, the seven albums could of course be shuffled in the box and different stickers (bits of old cover) made available to view through the central die cut hole – a sort of interactive, changeable box design.

▷ This circular cut out hole and the circular stickers provided the impetus for Peter Curzon's graphic design (see opposite) for the box itself. The very middle circle contains three elliptical discs, or flattened ovals (could they be UFOs on their sides?), representing 30 years of Pink Floyd. This motif was extended over all the liner bags to provide some cohesion to a project that had very little at the start.

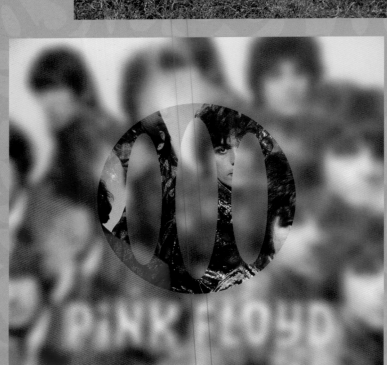

PINK FLOYD "The Piper At The Gates Of Dawn"
30th anniversary CD box [1997]

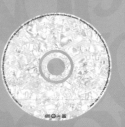

CATHERINE WHEEL "Little Muscle" CD single [1995]

Catherine Wheel's charming but obsessive lead singer Rob Dickinson wrote a song about the human tongue called 'Little Muscle', describing its versatility and extraordinary dexterity, simultaneously attractive and repellent. And he's right; the tongue is a strange thing indeed, sometimes revolting, as in the ear photo, or silly, as in tongues in the grass, or plain rude, or peculiar, as in chameleon tongue (see p131). This was an alternative design for Ragga (p121) and was an attempt at innovative packaging wherein the booklet would have an extra fold in the flap to extend the cover to three panels (there being three members of Ragga) which would be figuratively connected (like the music) but would contain separate images (the individual band characters). The tongue of the chameleon (in the middle)

becomes the water level of the submerging watch to the left, whilst to the right the chameleon's tail becomes the banisters of an ornate descending staircase. Three separate narratives connected not graphically or thematically but physically wherein the extension of one element transforms into an element of another. All very interesting, or so I thought, but it had little effect on the prospective client, namely Ragga. ▷ The rest of these next three pages contain further ideas which we thought were interesting but also had little effect on our clients. They remained unused, until now, and languished as rejects in the bowels of my chaotic studio. They are drawn up as pencil sketches, which are then coloured, usually with ordinary crayon. These roughs are devised to represent an idea or design which will be executed photographically in the end.

This cannot be done at first because it is simply too expensive, and very few clients would be prepared to cough up, and I don't blame them. Since the purpose is to show clearly what the content of the intended photograph is going to be, little or no attempt is made at representing the mood or style. We want to show the composition, the perspective, and the probable proportions, but not the colour, and particularly not the lighting.

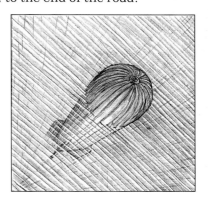

Roughs

What colouring we do is rudimentary and only there to serve the needs of content and meaning. The overall graphic quality as a cover is usually discernible whilst the rest of the many details are left to verbal explanation, and occasional photo reference, and to trust (as in …trust me, I'm a doctor). A client thus has a pretty good idea of what his or her cover design is going to be…which is, of course, no guarantee that they'll like it in the end (see p152). ◁

As you can readily see we have a mixed bunch of roughs but they represent only a small part of a larger collection (though not as large as it should be, or as others cynically think, because we forget to keep them, or fail to file them), including a road with a reversed perspective – so simple but so annoying. A kettle shape, which is described by a school of fish, probably different fish, which is in turn part of a sequence,

countryside to represent either giving 'a big hand' (as in audience clapping), or providing a helping hand (as in life, but not often enough I hear you say). A little sicker and more graphic is the naked couple standing at the unfinished edge of some motorway flyover construction, their relationship in tatters having come, as it were, to the end of the road.

including a human profile formed by a flock of birds in the air, of which the tree head (p115) is yet a further progression. Then there is the zeppelin ensnared by a layer of strings, and the half stone/half tree profile building thingy on a cliff edge which were designed for Kashmir Symphonic Led Zeppelin (p105). On a lighter note we have the octopus dress, which is worn as a fashion statement, the real octopus wrapped around a lovely woman like an elegant evening dress, and there is an enormous plaster hand being carried across the

▷ More graphic still is the constructivist like Thirties design from Jon Crossland for Ian Dury's album *Reasons To Be Cheerful*. 2B or not to be (below). The half bird man standing motionless like a heron in the reflective waters of an African lake is altogether more romantic, whereas the aerial view of the winding river in the jungle, with its graphic sexuality, is more simply a suggestive piece of design, conceived for an album whose title was *Eye To Eye*, fitting really well, so to speak, like the interlocking pieces of a jigsaw. I am fond of the cryptic political message of the rainforest design, suggesting that it is the avoidance of blame, the passing of the financial buck, which is a major contributor to the environmental fuck up: and of the psychological implication of the man on the analyst's couch subjected to extraordinary scrutiny of his inner processes and deeper motivations conducted not by a shrink but by some gigantic mechanical electrical probe the size of a spaceship. This is both threatening and complimentary…it takes such enormous technology to explore the enormous brain and equally enormous unconscious that we all have. ◁

Sometimes an image or graphic arrangement becomes fixated and I explore it many times over, and try desperately to sell it to someone so that I can do it for real. This version of infinite regression (p130) echoes *Ummagumma* (p161) but is based in fact on some Moorish doorways I saw in Seville, one through another, suggesting a receding set. I first tried the idea as a doorway, then turned it into circular porthole apertures and then into windows without glass, arranged at 90 degree angles to each other (45 degrees to the viewer). These windows are part of a real building, and one looks through a set of openings from inside a darkened room, across an alleyway, through another darkened room (in another wing as it were), and out into the park or countryside beyond. The final amendment was to change the inclination of the floors so that it became more like an Escher, or a fantasy world, where up and down were confused. My preference is probably for this version. It was regrettably nobody else's preference and remained unpublished, until now that is, obliged by fate to appear in my own book, where I can act as my own client – I can commission myself to commission myself to…

DREAM THEATER

Touring
Into
Infinity

97/98

DREAM THEATER

Touring
Into
Infinity
97/98

STEREOTOMY
INDUSTRIAL
VIDEOOFWOMEN ROBOT
CRISIS DARKSIDE
GAMBLING PYRAMID
POE
SURVEILLANCE
GREEDTOFLY
DESIRETOAUDI
ALAN
PARSONS
LIVE
PROJECT

SKUNKWORKS

Tour T-Shirts (clockwise from top left):
DREAM THEATER [1997/98]
SKUNKWORKS [1995]
ALAN PARSONS [1998]

The key to this garish extravaganza was verbal rather than visual. Instead of reacting to (or interpreting) the title *Just Add Life*, we conjured phrases that required the inclusion of the actual word 'life' to make them work. More literal than literal. Just add the word life, not life itself. For example 'Life's tough' or 'Life is sweet'. Or 'Life's a bitch', 'Life sucks', and 'Life is short'. Some more complex and demanding variations were thrown in to extend the intellectual boundaries a touch, namely 'A cat has nine lives', 'Life is not a bowl of cherries', even 'Life's rich tapestry'. But then we returned again to the direct no nonsense stuff like 'Life stinks', 'Life is sacred', and so on. We then elected to represent these verbal puns by suitable objects (sugar lump, cherries, dummy, etc) none of which would be arresting enough on their own, but which might work as a collection, especially if brightly presented. As such they would be more dynamic, and actually much more relevant to the music and attitude of the band. The Almighty concurred, so Rupert and Tony set about photographing these sundry small objects against a variety of strongly coloured backgrounds as seen opposite. The final arrangement of the objects in their neat little squares owed as much to the colour of their backgrounds as to the objects themselves, most of which were easily recognisable, if not a trifle silly. Jon Crossland dipped into his

ALMIGHTY

trash reserves and extracted some extremely loud but appropriate colours, logo style, and extended lozenge bars for the graphics of the package (see overleaf). I particularly liked the clashing solid colours of the vinyl liner bag, the washing detergent star drops (which I could swear he nicked from somewhere but he hotly denies it to this day), and the rounded corners he deployed for the separate photographic ingredients on the poster opposite, and on the front of the CD booklet.

▷ This was a fun job. No complex intellectual or psychological or emotional factors to carry, just up front no nonsense imagery, a brash attitude, bright OTT colours, and full of life. Two particular aspects merit further mention: the poster opposite which had an Escher like bulge, as if there were literally something pushing out from behind (which had to be artworked by the repro house (thank you Sonicon), and not ourselves because our measly computer at the time could not carry enough memory for this particular distortion). Also the CD jewel box which was made of heat reactive plastic – it's got a fancy name like thermatropic or something – but essentially it changes colour when heat is added, in this instance from bright green to yellow. If you held it firmly in your hand your grip would impart yellow finger prints to a green base (see next page). If you put the green jewel box on the radiator it would form yellow stripes, not that we recommend such a procedure of course. Just Add Life (ie heat) and things change, including the CD jewel case. What a trick! Gawd Almighty!

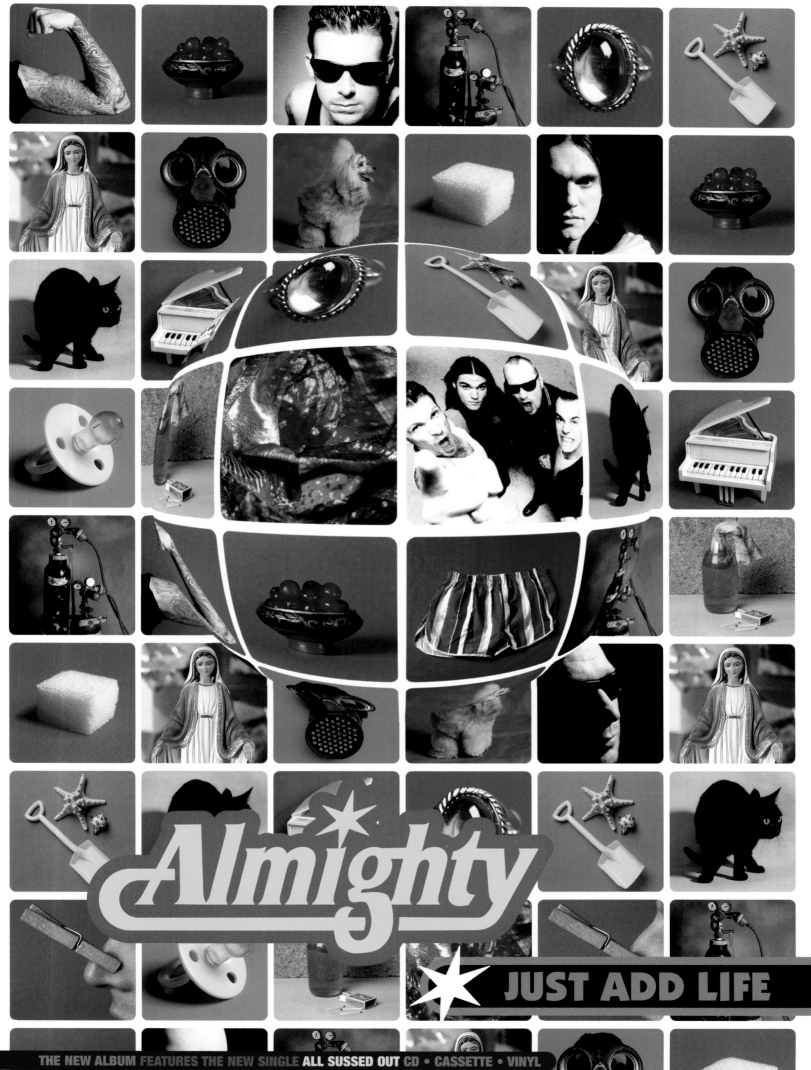

Almighty

★ **JUST ADD LIFE**

THE NEW ALBUM FEATURES THE NEW SINGLE **ALL SUSSED OUT** CD • CASSETTE • VINYL

INITIAL QUANTITIES OF THE CD & CASSETTE COME IN LIMITED EDITION COLOUR-CHANGING HEAT SENSITIVE BOXES

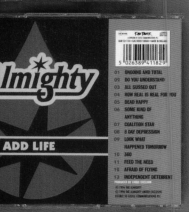

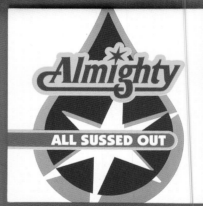

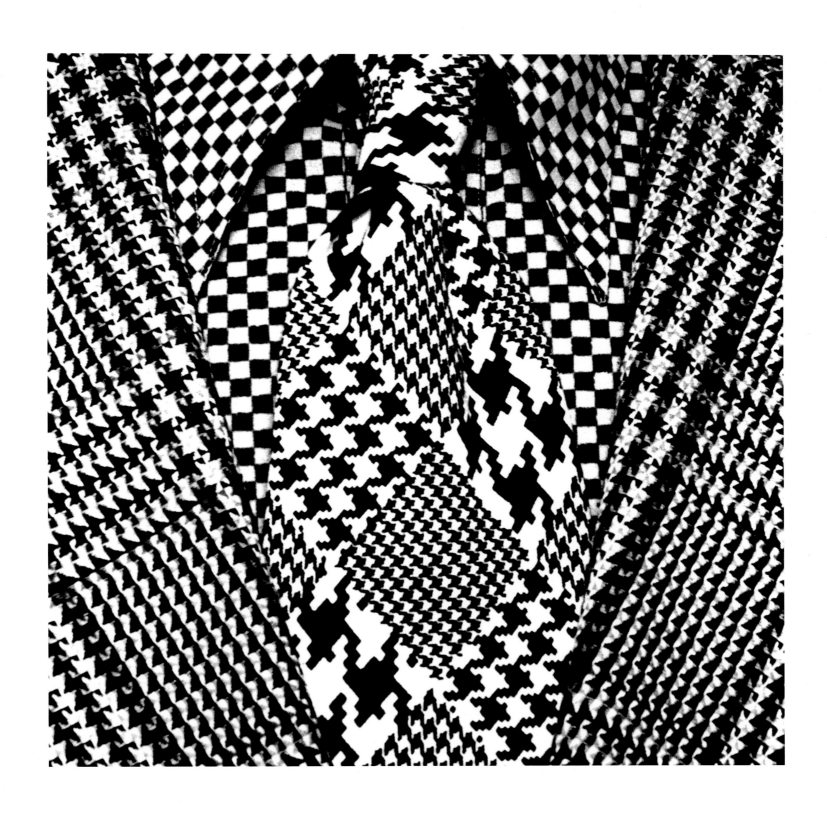

BILLY KARLOFF AND THE EXTREMES "Let Your Fingers Do The Talking" vinyl front [1982]

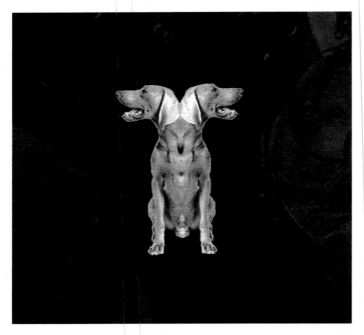

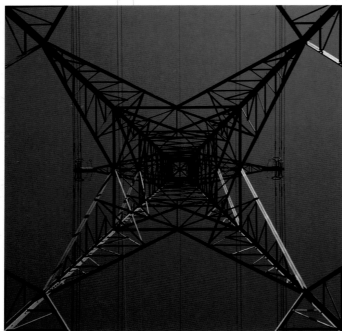

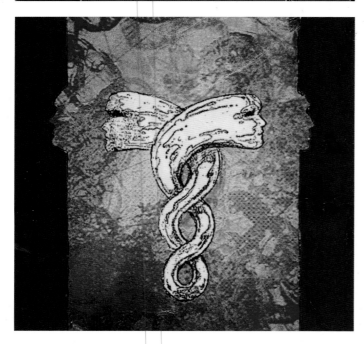

Mandalas, mirror images and symmetrical designs are as old as the hills. One finds them all over the natural world, not only as a general structural attribute (four legs, two eyes etc) but also in decoration and camouflage, especially in insects like butterflies. Not surprisingly man has mimicked nature and produced millions upon millions of variations across many cultures, especially in terms of decorative borders and Islamic patterns. Me and my colleagues tend to use it sparingly, and more as a metaphor, or where the mirror images combine to make a third different image, such as the techno industrial face opposite. The flopped mirror image of refinery pipes at a huge industrial complex turned 180 degrees looks like weird military headgear, or like the helmet of an American football player. The mandala of wrought iron superstructure on this page is actually an existing electric pylon seen from below from a perfectly central position. The two headed dog and the two headed serpent are attempts to represent the two faced quality of betrayal, and of history, looking both into the past and the future, like the Roman god Janus (January). The human serpent design is based, I think, upon an eclectic mixture of Uroborus, the Caduceus of healing, and a Moorish gargoyle I spotted once in Seville, neatly representing two things that come from one. Which is just another theme worthy of exploration and also as old as the hills.

▷ PS During some recent research into symbols and symbol history (for a book project) it struck me very forcibly that the mirror (or mirror image) is the key. Written symbols clearly differentiate man from all

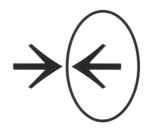

other animals. Written symbols differentiate modern man from his early predecessors. It is the written symbol which facilitated trade and civilisation, and provided the basis for science and technology. It is the written symbol which embodies extelligence – the passing and accumulation of information not via genes but outside the body via books and computers. It is the written symbol which looked back at early man and told him that he was thinking, and told other men that they too were thinking. The (written) symbol actualised thought, and enabled communication to expand rapidly. The symbol changed our lives. The symbol is the key to progress. Tribes without (written) symbols do not progress. And the symbol of symbols is a mirror, for the mirror looks back at us, as did the first written symbol, and told us that we were symbolising. The symbol for symbols, the ultimate symbol, should look like the above.

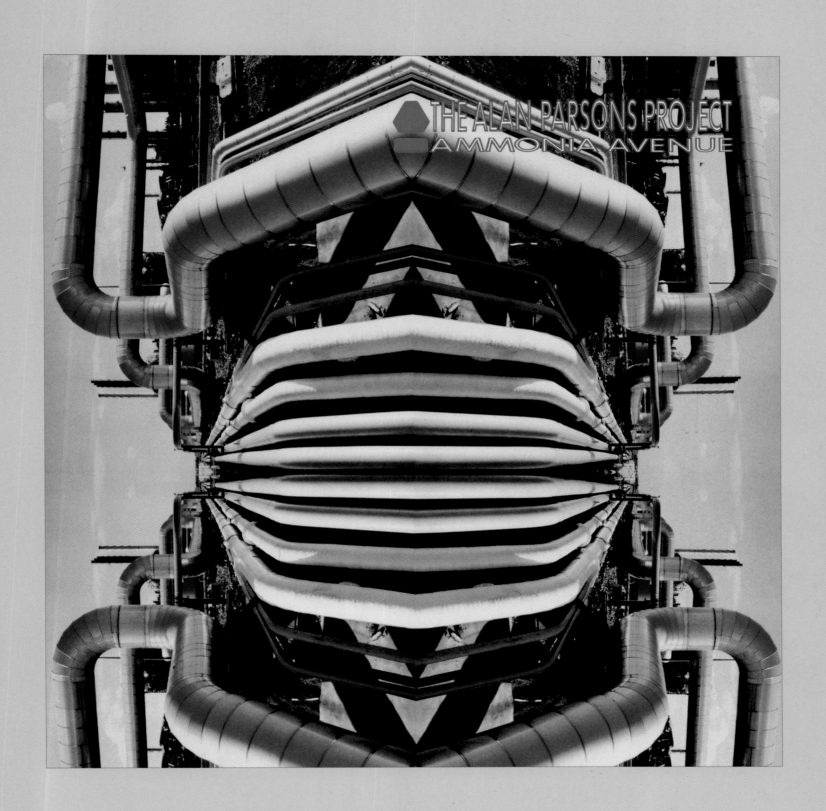

THE ALAN PARSONS PROJECT
AMMONIA AVENUE

TECHNO INDUSTRIAL

Gift To The Earth

The World Wildlife Fund's album *Gift To The Earth*, shown here, is a charity album. It may be unpopular to ask, but do such charity records work? If a bunch of musicians kindly donate tracks, ie waive royalties to an album collection so that (some of) the proceeds can go to the designated charity, is this the best way to help? Would charities benefit more, for example, by direct donation? Does the punter who buys the album have any idea what monies actually go to charity? Or what precise allocations are made and for what reasons? Is charity a good idea anyway? All these questions and more tend to permeate a project like *Gift To The Earth* which was organised by the very amiable Vic Coppersmith-Heaven, currently of ELF, previously of GWW (see p146) but on loan to WWF. He persuaded several recording artistes, and my good self, to donate our services free of charge. The design was

intended to embody the idea that all sorts of people from all walks of life could return something of their choice to the abused planet Earth. Big or small, money or object, plan or project, whatever one felt suitable. So we asked ourselves, what would the Earth like? What does it need? What would be an appropriate or symbolic gift? But we could not think of any single manageable thing. We fell back instead on the act of giving, ie a proffered hand, a helping

WORLD WILDLIFE FUND

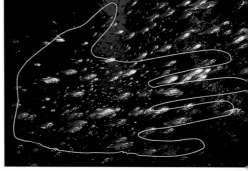

hand, bearing some kind of a gift. This gift would (symbolically) restore to the Earth what it was lacking, what man had taken away (forests, species, habitat, oxygen) and make it whole again, complete the picture, like the last piece of a jigsaw. This piece of jigsaw could be either a small object held in the outstretched hand (opposite) or a huge structure floating in space like an asteroid – an environmental island (top right). But this was of course expensive to construct, and the WWF were fearful that it would eat into the profit margins and defeat, in part, the object of the whole exercise. So we made a jigsaw shape of bamboo instead, symbolic of greenery and of forest replacement, and of food for the panda, long serving logo of the WWF. We made it bright green and bright red for both impact, and danger (our planet is in trouble) but it does not, I think, have the same impact as the floating island, being domestic not grand, graphic not imposing, effective but not so memorable. Don't mean to be uncharitable but that's how I see it…

John Peel

20
SHEELA-NA-GIG
PJ HARVEY
REC 23/10/91 MAIDA VALE 4
RECORDED BY MIKE ROBINSON & JAMES BIRTWISTLE
ROB - DRUMS
STEPHEN VAUGHAN - BASS GUITAR
PJ HARVEY - GUITAR/VOCALS

21
M64 THE BLACK EYE GALAXY
DAVE CLARKE AS DIRECTIONAL FORCE
REC 20/05/94 OWN STUDIO
DAVE CLARKE - DJ

22
THE BONG
DREADZONE
REC 21/08/94 MAIDA VALE 3
RECORDED BY MIKE ENGLES & STEVE BRIDGES
TIM BRAN - KEYBOARDS
GREG ROBERTS - DRUMS/SAMPLES
LEO WILLIAMS - BASS MASTER GENERAL
DAN DONOVAN - KEYBOARDS

23
JOHN CAGE BUBBLEGUM
STEREOLAB
REC 26/06/92 MAIDA VALE 3
RECORDED BY MIKE ENGLES & FRED KAY
TIM GANE - GUITAR
MARTIN KEAN - BASS
MICK CONROY - KEYS
ANDY RAMSEY - DRUMS
LAETITIA SADLER - VOCALS/KEYBOARDS
MARY HANSEN - VOCALS

12
GROOVY TRAIN
THE FARM
REC 06/05/90 MAIDA VALE 3
RECORDED BY DALE GRIFFEN & MIKE ENGELS
PETER HOOTON - LEAD VOCALS
STEVE GRIMES - GUITAR
CARL HUNTER - BASS GUITAR
KEITH MULLIN - GUITAR/BACKING VOCALS
RAY BOULTER - DRUMS
BEN LEACH - KEYBOARDS

13
YOU'LL NEVER WALK ALONE
SHAMBEKO! SAY WAH
REC 05/05/82 MAIDA VALE 4
RECORDED BY ROGER PUSEY & NICK GOMM
PETE WYLIE - (EVERYTHING!!! EXCEPT
ODDBALL WASHINGTON BASS GUITAR

14
KIMBLE
THE FALL
REC 19/01/92 MAIDA VALE 3
RECORDED BY DALE GRIFFEN, MIKE ENGELS, JAMES
BIRTWISTLE
SIMON WOOLSTENCROFT - DRUMS
STEPHEN HANLEY - BASS GUITAR
CRAIG SCANLON - GUITAR
DAVID BUSH - KEYBOARDS
MARK E SMITH - VOCALS

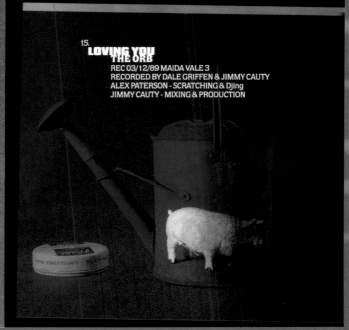

15
LOVING YOU
THE ORB
REC 03/12/89 MAIDA VALE 3
RECORDED BY DALE GRIFFEN & JIMMY CAUTY
ALEX PATERSON - SCRATCHING & DJing
JIMMY CAUTY - MIXING & PRODUCTION

30
SESSIONS
OF
PEEL
'67 '97

JOHN PEEL "30th Anniversary Commemorative Album" CD 1 front cover

overleaf: CD 2 front cover

JOHN PEEL

John Peel is a phenomenon. In the everchanging, fashion conscious, ephemeral world of popular music very few things last. John Peel has lasted. He has been a radio DJ for longer than anyone can remember. And he has had credibility for more years than is credible. And he has stayed true to his beliefs in exposing new and little heard music – music he personally likes. To commemorate 30 years of this unlikely phenomenon BBC Radio One wanted to present him with something special and unique, an idiosyncratic equivalent of a gold watch. They decided to give him an album, in fact a double album, of 30 of his favourite radio sessions – but in the form of an actual CD. A one off CD, which would look like a real CD that could be bought from any record shop, and which would of course need a cover design. Two CDs, two sides of John Peel. One side refined, one side rough and ready. One respectful and thoughtful, the other aggressive and cheeky. You can guess, surely, which side of his character this image represents. If you can't you're a twit. Blah!

(Figures In) Landscapes

Do you ever look in the mirror and wonder if you're stark raving mad? Or just common or garden crazy? If you make pictures for a living they can act like mirrors. They can tell you sometimes if you're mad, especially if you look at them later on, like this image opposite. It was conceived for a trio of Sixties and Seventies reprobates called Gentlemen Without Weapons (an overstated name I fear) for their album of pro-environmental musical ditties, offering advice and admonishment for a better world. (GWW later became ELF – Earth Love Fund – a full blown environment charity doing rainforesty things in Brazil, Central America and Indonesia, and recognised and awarded by the United Nations for sterling efforts, (see p141).) Kenny Young, Nick Glennie-Smith and Vic Coppersmith-Heaven called their album *Transmissions* –

messages to a beleaguered world – and wanted me to design an album cover, later to make a video for a single, 'Spirit Of The Forest', and a documentary about various celebrities who took part (but that is another story). The entire proposition was charity led – raising money to help the environment – which in

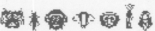

turn poses awkward questions. How much does one charge if anything? Does charity work in a society like ours? Is it desirable (politically speaking), practical, or just a sop? It's very hard to be critical and not respectful for fear of criticism from others. I am critical, but yet I took part anyway and donated my time on a charitable basis...but that too is another story (see p141). ◁ The idea was to suggest a curious but special way of transmitting the message rather than what the message actually was. The latter could leave one open, I felt, to obvious criticism, either about content, or about proselytising. The idea also derived from the notion that thoughts rather than deeds, mental

messages rather than verbal ones, might be preferable – a sort of scientific 'good vibes': in effect, the harnessing of brainwaves in an orderly and useful fashion, specifically to save the environment. Thus there are people sitting on little platforms, on the high poles, transmitting their thoughts in an endless line – pylons across the countryside – perched high to avoid ground interference, like radio masts. I thought the effect of this image would be weakened if I faked it (again this is pre-computer), so I staged it for real – real poles in a real field.

▷ When I look again at this picture, I think I must be a bit crazy, because it was such a nightmare to produce. Doing it for real, my avowed philosophy, necessitated huge wooden telegraph poles (20 of them, which in turn required locating and transporting them), bulldozers, pile drivers, and teams of rugged chaps to help erect the poles in conditions – not that you'd know looking at the end result – which were truly abysmal, comprising acres of wet slushy mud. Whichever memory I dredge up serves only to confirm the suspicion of implicit madness, be it the awkwardness and sheer weight of the poles, or the bad tempered farmer who doubled his location price the night before the shoot; be it digging holes deep enough for the poles to remain erect, or persuading luckless friends and models that they were perfectly safe sitting on top (and how they couldn't die of exposure or vertigo), and for what? All for a band with an overstated name, mixed motives, lofty ideals, no financial profit, and a shitload of aggravation. Just as well I like the environment. Just as well I like the image, or I'd know for sure that I was bonkers.

GENTLEMEN WITHOUT WEAPONS "Transmissions" vinyl front [1988]

One doesn't want to be accused of being pig headed, oh no, but there are times when one needs to stay firm, stick to one's guns and follow one's convictions. This cover design was just such an occasion. It was for a record called *In The Spirit* by the concept post psychedelic band Kansas, who had one huge album called *Point Of No Return* with a richly illustrated cover of a waterfall in the middle of the sea over which a boat was pitching. *In The Spirit*, however, required complex photography and very controlled circumstances, ie in a studio or interior location, with plenty of electricity, and no extraneous problems like wind or rain, but Kansas thought otherwise. The original design was set in a bar late at night and involved the spirit forms of listless habitués, lonely travellers of the urban night-time, absorbed in memories of their younger selves. Kansas liked the idea but not the setting. ◁

They flew me to…Kansas, to hang with them and discuss details. They wanted the location to be outdoors not indoors. I don't really understand why I gave way and didn't stick to my guns, but I didn't…and I wish I had. The whole affair came about shortly after the dramatic demise of my previous company, called Green Back Films, which involved near bankruptcy, separated partners and a crippling loss of confidence. It took three years of hard endeavour to discharge my debts and regain some composure, and the Kansas job occurred during that period. Understandable then that I might concede, but not really forgivable, because the result is forever staring me in the face (see opposite). Unforgivable too because I was already familiar with the intricate technique and knew full well what was most needed. As if by divine punishment this job was also cursed by personality clashes of tedious and ugly proportions, by fractious relations with the record company, and finally by the band who felt lukewarm about the outcome. Not that I blame them. Either I should have fought them, and insisted on my way of doing things, or alternatively…no, there's no

alternative in this instance: I think I should have done what I knew to be best.

▷ The idea for this cover was to represent the younger spirits of two older people, whose love was now dried up but whose previous (younger) love had been fresh and vibrant – young lovers reaching out for each other hungrily, keen and eager to be together. The older selves are indifferent and separate, too disenchanted to make reparation. I like the idea and in theory the technique was very suitable: it's just that the exterior location screwed the whole thing up, especially the central issue of the lighting. The technique required that the older figures remain completely still during a time exposure to produce a sharp image, which is a much easier task sitting on stools in some interior bar or café in the day, rather than standing outside in the middle of the night, freezing their butts off.

▷ Back to the technique. It's intriguing. Look closely. Have you any idea what is going on? The effect of distorted and elongated ghostly bodies might not be so difficult via your modern computer, but this is pre computer times. No trickery here. It's all done in the camera, though what you see is nothing like what you get. This is a picture taken over time, using a technique called slitscan photography. The elongation is caused by the movement of the white figure slowly round the stationary figure. This is captured not by slow shutter speed, as in photos of blurred tail lights, but by a moving light, a thin horizontal slit of light from a powerful projector which descends the frame passing slowly over the white figure. The shutter is in fact left open (which is why the overall scene must be dark, ie night-time) and the white figure exposes where and when the slit of light catches, which is of course determined by the movement. As the figure moves through space across the frame, it exposes along its path. The nearer figure, for example, started out in front and to the right of the standing woman, and slowly moved round, clockwise and behind, then reached out towards the other white figure. The two white figures (young lovers) rehearsed their movement in

KANSAS

relation to the timing of the slit of light passing from top to bottom so that they knew at what speed to move to make the shapes desired, ie ghostly shapes which encircled the older stationary figures. The exposure time of the slit of light on the moving figures must match that of all the combined light falling on the rest of the scene to avoid any over exposure. All in all a complex business, which can certainly deliver the goods if performed in controlled surroundings, but not out in the sticks, on some beaten up old farm, in the cold Californian night.

KANSAS "In The Spirit" CD front [1988]

ALAN PARSONS "Try Anything Once" vinyl front [1993]

There's a location down in Spain that I just love. We found it whilst making a commercial back in 1990. Strangely this worked out fine, given that I'm normally not too keen on commercials, nor they on me. It was shown repeatedly during World Cup '90 and its only drawback was the product that it was promoting, which is often, if not always, the case with commercials. All that effort, all that artistry, all that money, and for what? To persuade you to be interested in products which are uninteresting in themselves and basically similar despite what the commercial tries so hard to tell you. In this case the product was sugar. Ouch! All my industry devoted to saying that sugar is natural and all right for human consumption. The only defence I could muster was that the ad was, in essence, too stupid to be credible. I actually believed that the vast majority of people out there in consumer-land would know that the premise was bullshit. Nobody in their right mind could possibly believe that sugar, white sugar at that, was all right. Not the best argument I ever conceived but enough to permit me to shoot a good looking commercial and make 20K to get me out of debt. ◁

But I digress. The location was special and secret – photographers have favourite locations like favourite models, and pretend that nobody else knows about them: but I'm going to tell you anyway. It's 30 miles east of Jaen, which is between Madrid and Granada (nearer the latter), and consists of a wide valley

between two small ranges at the edge of the Sierra Nevada. This valley contains undulating fields, volcanic mounds, perfectly round hillocks like pert breasts, a single railway line with an empty station, deserted farmhouses, and a fairytale village of white houses clustered round the base of an isolated green mountain. The village is called Larva, hence the location came to be known as Larva Valley, and it is truly a magical place. We nearly opted for a perfect glacial valley in the Lake District, but decided in favour of Spain because of the light and the variety of spectacular scenery in the same vicinity.

▷ As for these guys hanging around this beautiful location, I am at a loss for a reasonable explanation. Is it some obscure (mental) group who meet under special circumstances? Suited like a board meeting and

THE THREE OF ME

THERE'S A VOICE ON THE PHONE
WHO JUST CALLED IN TO SAY
"MR JONES ISN'T HOME
HE'LL BE GONE FOR THE DAY"

SO HE PULLS DOWN THE BLIND
TO ADJUST HIS DISGUISE
BUT IT'S ALL IN HIS MIND
WHICH HE PROUDLY DENIES

I TURN THE BOAT BACK FROM THE WEIR
WHERE TO GO FROM HERE
I CAN'T HIDE FROM EACH FACE I SEE
LOOKING OUT FROM BEHIND THEM IS ME

I'M ATTEMPTING TO GUESS
WHAT THEY MEANT WHEN THEY SAID
"MR JONES AND HIS GUEST
WON'T BE USING THE BED"

SO IF I TAKE THE RAP
WHILE THEY STAY OUT OF SIGHT
I CAN SPRING FROM THE TRAP
WHEN THE TIMING IS RIGHT

ONE MINUTE I THINK I KNOW WHAT I MEAN
THE NEXT I HEAR VOICES INSIDE DISAGREE
WHY ARE THEY LAUGHING AT ME?

SO I PICK UP THE PHONE
SOMEONE'S ASKING OF ME
IS THE REAL MISTER JONES
MISTER ONE, TWO OR THREE?

SO I SAY THAT THEY'RE NOT
BUT IT'S NOT AS I SAY
'COS THEY'RE ALL THAT I'VE GOT
AND I CAN'T GET AWAY

AND ALICE WAVES US THROUGH THE GLASS
ARE WE HOME AT LAST
FOR TOMORROW THEY'LL BE HERE YOU SEE
LOCKED AWAY SAFE INSIDE THERE WITH ME

'COS TOMORROW THEY'LL BE HERE YOU'LL SEE
LOCKED AWAY SAFE INSIDE THEY'RE WITH ME

ONE MINUTE I THINK I KNOW WHAT I MEAN
THE NEXT I HEAR VOICES INSIDE DISAGREE
WHY ARE THEY LAUGHING AT ME?

THE THREE OF ME

(PACK/POWELL)

DAVID PACK
VOCALS, SYNTHS, GUITARS
STUART ELLIOTT
DRUMS
ANDREW POWELL
BASS, SYNTHS
IAN BAIRNSON
GUITARS
RICHARD COTTLE
SYNTHS
GRAHAM PRESKETT
VIOLINS

hanging upside down to increase blood to the brain? Perhaps it's a think tank. Or some kind of torture, but nobody looks that distressed. It could be a bizarre ritual in which diverse offerings are brought to the table, so to speak, and secrets are exchanged. None of these reasons accounts in any way for the group of harlequins hanging around in the distance. All I can say is that the mind works in a mysterious way – especially when hung upside down. In my heart of hearts, I suspect it was computer courtship, early days in the digital love affair in which things previously impossible or very difficult became easier and more convincing. For example, ropes hanging from the skies, endlessly long ropes stretching up to God knows where, lowering sky dwellers down for a visit. Crazy sky tourists getting a buzz. They'll try anything, those sky people. This is certainly not something to be attempted at home.

ALAN PARSONS / TRY ANYTHING ONCE

'*Don't get mad*, get even' is the battle cry of vengeful wives who have been cheated upon by their husbands. Although revenge is often cited as a silly, immature motive, it is more complex than expected, very human and occasionally quite useful. Us graphic designers rarely have the chance for revenge, being mere hired hands at the beck and call of egotistical rock stars, brutalising managers and inept record companies amongst others. We are rarely valued enough (boo hoo) to get power because it is, after all, the music which matters and album design doesn't affect record sales, well, not that anyone will openly admit. We don't often get the chance to tell bands or record companies to do what we say, or seek much redress when summarily dismissed. Not much chance for revenge. BUT HERE GOES. ◁

Wishbone Ash were a twin guitar band of the Seventies. *Melody Maker*'s band of the year back in '72. They made several albums but were never that successful. Toured regularly, but failed to make a mark. Twenty-five years later leader Andy Powell is still propelling Wishbone Ash round occasional tours and the odd record release. Hamburg's Repertoire Records make a reasonable living from re-releasing obscure but carefully chosen old material, and re-packaging it appropriately (see p170). Repertoire commissioned Andy to do a four record set, *Best Of Wishbone*, and all agreed I should do the cover, including me. I met Andy (after 20 years I might add) in my local café, and was visited shortly thereafter by an image in the mind scanner, clear cut and complete. It even came with a title 'Twin Rivers', after twin guitars, and *Twin Peaks*. ◁

On this page is a rough of the idea of one river temporarily dividing into two, seen from the air, containing naked male swimmers – 'boys playing together in the rivers of their female creativity'. It felt an acutely appropriate image, despite being enormously difficult to shoot. I rang Andy with enthusiasm, faxed him the rough, and told him how thrilled I was. "Doesn't it look a little rude and provocative?" Andy enquired. I assured him that of course it did, but it wasn't really – it was an aerial photograph of a dividing river, and he should always say that in interviews. It was the truth. It might certainly look vaginal and possibly provocative, but

that's art, isn't it? That's rock 'n' roll. Andy said okay and the record company said okay, so we embarked upon yet another complete production nightmare.

▷ It was October turning to November, cold and grey. It took us weeks to find a location near enough to London to be economic. We had to arrange a helicopter test for both photographic reasons and helicopter safety, and then we had to repeat it all for real during very changeable British weather. Tony May loved it, being a helicopter freak, but the swimmers hated it, because the river was spring fed and was the second coldest river in Southern England, which was none too warm at that time of year anyway. The helicopter needed to maintain a position 300ft above the river bend, whilst Tony lent out into mid air to shoot, and the swimmers swam in the freezing water below dying of hypothermia.

▷ And then Andy rejected the finished design. He said it was too rude, and that it was unfavourable to women. He claimed it did, in fact, look too much like a vagina, which was 'uncool', and would get the band into trouble. Couldn't hack it, eh, Andy? Can't take a bit of trouble? It's all rock 'n' roll isn't it? Sex and controversy. The rumour was that his wife didn't approve of the design, so what's her problem? Doesn't like her own genitalia? He sent me some stupid letter telling me again that it was insulting because it looked like a vagina, and I faxed him back in a furious fashion asking if he really believed that vaginas were bright green and blue, and had people swimming in them? That the image is suggestive – young males swim up giant vaginal river – is true: in fact it's quite common in the visual arts to be suggestive, and therefore nothing to get into a lather about. Our picture was always a real event, a geographical event, figures in a landscape, swimming up a wet river, bordered by fields and green trees. It cannot *be* a vagina; it can only allude to one.

▷ The question I ask myself, trying to restrain my anger and not appear more mad than usual, is as follows: does this episode tell me that my design was really disrespectful to women? Or simply not very good? Or does it tell me that Wishbone Ash lack the courage to follow their convictions? Not enough balls perhaps, never mind vaginas.

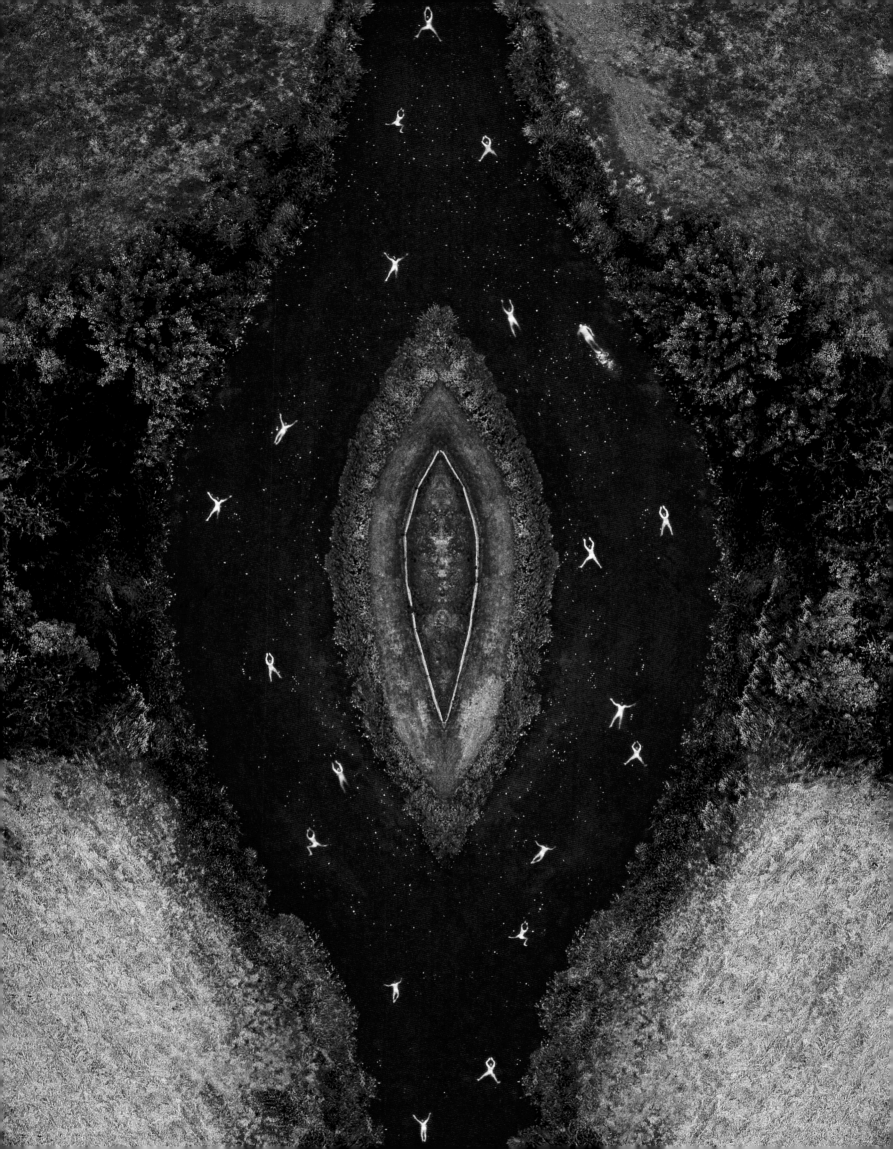

BRUCE DICKINSON
SKUNKWORKS

Bruce Dickinson, of Iron Maiden fame, fencing expert, author and all round sharp geezer, reminded me that Skunkworks was not only the name of his then new band, but also of the secret American research outfit cum task force principally responsible for advanced aircraft technology, but also telepathic experiments, virtual weaponry, and whose alleged remit included absolute secrecy especially, of course, in relation to UFOs and transport systems developed in co-operation with aliens. With this in mind, but without telling a soul, one of the ideas submitted to Bruce included a man standing beneath a small tree, whose close clipped hedge like foliage was shaped like a brain. It was a brain tree (there is a village 50 miles ENE of London called Braintree. I thought you should know that). This motif represented in a poetic fashion the research element of Skunkworks. Their secret nature, on the other hand, was to be indicated by 'a hidden face' – the contours of the water's edge would form the outline of one side of a face which would be flipped and joined together to provide a whole face, whilst boulders in the water might give the impression of the eyes, nose and mouth of the said hidden face. This is all loosely speaking, and would only be visible if you were to look hard. It would not be really there but would be 'secret', like the activities of Skunkworks. On opposite promontories would stand two solitary men, each with his own brain tree, so tailor made it looked as though his complex thinking had shaped it. ◁

This verbal guff is all very well, but how was the idea, the image to be realised? We decided to make our own tree and take it with us – that's the kind of people we are – to the actual location itself, but where was that? We needed water and a small-scale irregular shoreline in order to flip and recombine to form a face like mirror image – the 'hidden face'. Sounds simple enough, but none of us had a clue: local ponds, rivers, lakes appeared useless when tested. Eventually, out of desperation as much as inspiration, we ended up on Rannoch Moor in Scotland, just south of Glencoe. I say 'we' but I didn't go. Tony, Rupert and Peter went along with Alton Omer as model and tree carrier. By all accounts they had a mixed time of it. Great location, freezing cold, and completely changeable weather, veering from bright sunlight to thick mist in an hour or two, and back again just as quick. Either the awkwardness of the required shoreline, or the biting cold, or forgetfulness or some other brain lapse meant they didn't return with all the necessary pictures. No suitable shoreline. "So much for the brain tree," I quipped in my anger and frustration. "Didn't seem to do you lot any good – where's my face?" No hidden face to form when the picture was flipped and joined. So much for half the idea. No reference to secrecy. What would Mr Dickinson say about that?

▷ However, half a good idea is better than none, as I realised when my anger abated. What I also realised is that the brain tree was kind of cool: stark and curious, stuck out there in the middle of a bleak nowhere. And when the picture was mirrored it suggested some strange ritual, or an assignation of brains, a meeting of minds. Unlike the cot image on p65 the location is redeeming, but even more particularly the photograph itself is very special, with its spectral centre light lending an ethereal quality as if lit from within, making the image look peaceful and disturbing, reflective and moody, all at the same time. It's a great shot and more than compensates for the hidden face, now so hidden it's been forgotten.

▷ It all goes to prove that half a good idea is better than a whole poor idea, and that a good idea needs to be presented with skill and artistry. Indifferent technique can impair a good idea, that's for sure. What is not so clear is whether great technique can save a poor idea. I have my doubts. Moderate technique for a moderate idea is, well, kind of moderate. Good realisation of a good idea, that's what I say, and I'm sure that's what they say down at Skunkworks. If they exist, of course.

BRUCE DICKINSON "Skunkworks" CD front [1996]

The Cranberries have a great story to tell about how they became successful without knowing it: imprisoned on a bus tour of Eastern Europe, schlepping round grim cities with other bands on an hysterical merry go round of music and mirth, their first single was released without publicity and promptly sold millions in the States, catapulting them overnight from obscurity to limelight.

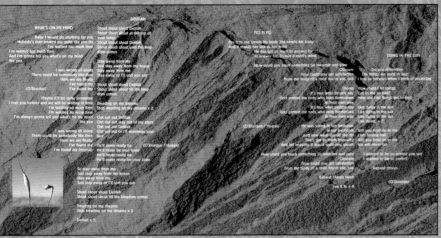

Lead singer Dolores also has great but harrowing tales to tell of her own life, and episodes from these form the backbone of many of her songs. She most particularly likes to know where you stand. "You see, Storm," she explained intensely, "I'm either committed or I'm not. I love you or I hate you. You're either with me or you're not. Black or white, that's how I am." Of course recollection tends to simplify things but this polarity is a central part of Dolores, of her songs, and of Cranberry music. She moves like a butterfly, stings like a bee: tender and assertive by turn, and wonderfully sarcastic, invoking harsh or damning indictment in the sweetest of voices. Positive or negative, she's with you or against you. No half measures in the Cranberry cosmos, at least not too many. ◁

Two sides of The Cranberries, two sides of a story, and so two images for a cover design. One paranoid and the other confident. One cowering, one fighting back, standing tall. The hovering, robotic, all seeing eye of psychic guilt, or of unnamed government agencies (see opposite), pins our vulnerable naked selves to the floor, where we cover our heads to hide, but we cannot escape, even in the furthest reaches of a barren landscape. So what we gotta do is fight back, stand up, tell the great eye of intrusion to get the fuck out of there, be gone from our lives! The robotic eye is shocked, of course, and jumps back in amazement, its eyelashes pulled back sharply, its lids wide open in surprise (see p157). ◁

This little parable, this affirming anti-paranoid diptych, then appeared either side of an ordinary CD jewel box, but with a trompe l'oeil repeat of the side front panel (the tray) on the back inlay card, making the back of the box look, at a glance, the same as the front (d'ya follow?). The Cranberries then insisted that there was no bar code, no

THE CRANBERRIES - BURY THE HATCHET

legal lines or writing of any kind so that, in effect, front and back were identical and interchangeable. Radical and revolutionary, at least in packaging terms, not even PF and LZ had managed this. I guess it all fits in with Dolores' character – either there is writing or there isn't. "Who the fuck cares," she declared angrily, "for business legal record company crap?" The information, including the dreaded bar code, was cut to a minimum and put on peelable stickers, affixed either side of the box. This procedure (detested of course by the record company) lent further weight to the illusion that the plastic jewel box had two fronts, or no back, which in fact meant half the time one attempted to open it on the wrong side, ie from the back (which was disguised as a front). All very confusing at first, but enjoyably irritating, especially watching the uninitiated trying to figure out why they couldn't open the box. (This could of course infuriate some punters, but Dolores was equally scathing about them. "There will, of course," she jibed, "be some old miseries out there who won't enjoy a little joke!")

▷ The shoot in Arizona was appropriately two sided, lurching from high farce to near despair. The robotic eye was unexpectedly expensive to freight and very troublesome to transport. When we arrived in Flagstaff it

actually snowed. Couldn't believe it. Miraculously the weather cleared further north, providing two glorious days of perfect winter light. On location on the first morning our truck broke down in the middle of nowhere. We got the Navaho heebie jeebies about working on what might be sacred land, and with what exactly? An evil eye and a naked man! Should be easy to explain. And then we were caught speeding twice (that's Andy Earl for you, photographer to the stars, father of two and speed freak). But the weather stayed good, the location was fantastic, and the nude model behaved very well. Which is more than I could say for the hovering eye which, in my fantasy, got fed up with all the photography and being put away in its box time and again and so escaped, went fly about, looking for fresh victims to intimidate. It's probably watching you now, as you read these words.

opposite: THE CRANBERRIES "Bury The Hatchet" CD front [1999]

opposite:

THE CRANBERRIES "Bury The Hatchet" poster [1999]

THE CRANBERRIES

BURY THE HATCHET

DREAM THEATER "Falling Into Infinity" cassette front [1997]

DREAM THEATER

This design emerged from eclectic sources susceptible on this occasion to identification. First there was the cobbled Eastern philosophy from hippy days, which recalls the watcher, or seer, who sees all things. There was the paranoia from 20th century urban living, and a fucked up childhood, wherein we think we are being continually watched. Then there was a television advert for four wheel drive macho vehicles, now used by upper middle class mums for the school run, which included 'watching towers', and finally there was a Gary Larson 'Far Side' cartoon of a huge bird eating a birdwatcher, seen through the binoculars of another birdwatcher, who may well be its next victim. Add to this brew the graphic attraction of the binocular semi-circles set snugly in a square through which the action is surveyed, plus the geometric nature of the constituents that make up the entire design, and you have a complete image. You have what you see opposite, close indeed to the original rough which first crept forth from the brain soup.

Dream Theater hail from New York and from an unashamedly bygone age of progressive rock which they purvey regularly on tour across the land with a vigour and a degree of support I would not have anticipated. In addition they were very charming, and great to work with, ie full of compliments and well organised. Graphic designers have frail egos too: it's not the private preserve of musicians, you know. We need compliments, we need love. I think they selected this design (out of several) because of the title, since there is potentially an infinity, albeit of regression, ie who is watching who is watching who etc. A regressive infinity is better than no infinity at all, is what I say. The

same principle underlies a design I made for Pink Floyd back in 1969, called *Ummagumma*, although it was represented literally back then. The Dream Theater image is, however, more conceptual.

▷ A purpose built computer, namely a Diacormid system (better than Paintbox or Mamba, more powerful than a Mac), was used to make this image. Not only for obvious details, like the black out of focus front binocular graphic, but also for other important items, like the tiny binoculars tilted at the right angle for the watchers (so as to look directly at each other), or moving one watcher more centrally on his little platform, plus cleaning the poles of the towers and brightening their reflections in the water. To show just how scandalous things can really get I'll own up to there being only one tower in reality, and only one person, who was in fact photographed twice – he just sat the other way round and wore different clothes. He was positioned in the correct part of the lens over to one side, so that each tower, each exposure was the right perspective when recombined. Since the two pictures were taken from the same camera position they were very easy to join in the computer. Another image utilised in the package (for which this main image is the front), is an out of focus photograph of the watcher on his tower. One knows what it is yet

somehow it looks different. In fact, it's a weeny bit suggestive, a little phallic even, which is to the taste of some like Dream Theater but not to others like Wishbone Ash. It's all in the eye of the beholder, or as in this instance, the eye of the watcher.

Fritz Kreisler played wonderful classical violin throughout the Twenties and Thirties. He was a virtuoso much admired by musicians and public alike. Not only did he perform brilliantly, but he also composed numerous pieces, many in the baroque style. Two particular aspects marked him out. Firstly, he played like an angel: secondly he composed pieces but pretended they were not his own. He attributed them instead to obscure (and sometimes fictitious) baroque composers. Amazing. He claimed that in this way he could insert them into his concert programme without disturbance. Credit was not the issue. Kreisler was not 'unmasked' for some 20 years; instead audiences simply enjoyed the pieces and loved his playing. ◁

At the other end of the violin spectrum is the one and only (thank God) Nigel Kennedy – modern phenomenon, enfant terrible, soccer crazy, hard drinking genius, seemingly sharing with Kreisler only one quality – the ability to play beautifully. ◁ Nigel, however, saw himself in other ways similar to Kreisler, not in terms of professional stature, more in terms of societal position. He made an album of Kreisler tunes and favourite concert pieces called *Kindred Spirit*. And it was fantastic: truly a beautiful thing. We began to work together on the album cover, and on a TV film project care of 'Chips' Chipperfield, not of circus lineage, which was in fact our second attempt at co-operation. Previously we had concocted a set of videos for Vivaldi's *Four Seasons*, not of hotel lineage, called modestly *Corridors Of The Mind* ('Corrida Degli Spiriti' sounded much better), but this was cast aside in favour of a live performance.

I didn't expect to be rejected again. ◁

But how wrong can you be! We worked hard trying to unravel Nigel's thoughts apropos a TV documentary (with dramatic vignettes) walking across the Malvern Hills where Vaughan Williams, or was it William Walton, had once walked, near Nigel's country retreat. (If you had seen his town gaff you'd know why he needed a country retreat.) Meanwhile I designed the album cover around the twin muses in Kreisler's life – playing and composing – and pictured them as female shapes, or silhouettes (in deference also to the two major women in his life). They were connected to the one source, Kreisler himself, by means of strings – strings of the violin, of course, but also strings of attachment, strings of commitment. The whole image was intended to be minimal, geometric and elegant. A dash of mystery perhaps, but mostly cool and classical. Tony May took an excellent photo at Camber Sands on the South Coast of England late in the afternoon, with perfect winter

sun. We loved it. Nigel said he loved it. I asked graphic pal Rob O'Connor of Stylorouge to execute the artwork. He agreed. What could go wrong?

▷ Once bitten twice shy. I should've known that Nigel is frighteningly unpredictable. I'd worked with him before. And what he did was unpredictably unpredictable. He completed the album, but decided that he didn't, on reflection, want to release it at all. "Old style," he asserted. "It gets in the way of my new shit, man" – violin interpretations of Jimi Hendrix. The cover was finished, and even proofed, but the record itself was shelved indefinitely. Such a shame for me, but more so for other folks, who didn't get to hear Kennedy playing Kreisler. Oh Nigel, child in adult's clothing, brilliant violinist, champagne scoffer, Aston Villa fanatic, spouter of expletives, media aggressive, self confessed wild man of classical rock, why did you do that? And then in '98, just as predictably, he changed his mind and released the album after all. However he replaced my picture with a photo of himself, the swine, which was pretty depressing – but quite predictable.

NIGEL KENNEDY "Kindred Spirit" vinyl front [1995]

Why don't record companies make promo videos that relate to record covers? Or have record covers which relate to videos? Why don't rock 'n' roll managers encourage their bands to connect the promotional material? These 'captains of industry' spend enough time insisting on other branding, and on big type, clean labelling, bar codes and catalogue numbers, why can't they get their heads round this one? ◁

There clearly seems to be some link between the cover designs and the videos. Both items are trying to represent the music, trying to use the visual medium to promote the product. If an image, or a figure, is used on, say, a single bag, why can't it be repeated, albeit briefly, in the video? An echo here or there to reinforce the promotion, exercised with restraint if necessary. It makes sense, but it doesn't happen much. ◁

I strongly suspect that this is because the 'captains of commerce' see covers and videos entirely differently. Videos are simply and primarily promotional items. Videos (TV exposure) can make a band, or break a single. Album covers (and single bags) are…well, decorative perhaps, a sales tool, informative even, but neither one thing nor the other really, and are not so important anyhow. Perhaps record companies are right, in commercial terms – they certainly throw much more money at videos – but not in artistic terms. Certainly not in durability. There are, to be sure, some great videos, but by and large they are restricted by promotional criteria and broadcast policies. Too much plastic personality and predictable performance. Too much TV interruption, or shortening, or worst of all, the showing of excerpts called 'clips'. Poor video directors. How can they function creatively under such constraints? Well, what they often do is make videos that are fast, repetitive and meaningless, to allow for 'clippability' and the pedestrian demands of promotion. As Kevin Godley pointed out, it's such a shame since videos offer a great chance to fuse music and imagery into a piece of art instead of disposable rubbish. ◁

But enough of this tubthumping, though it's not entirely unrelated. These images for Alan Parsons, of Alan Parsons Project fame, and *Dark Side* engineer

ALAN PARSONS

fame, and sundry producer fame, were devised firstly for a video that we shot in California for a song called 'Turn It Up', which was from the album *Try Anything Once*. We had in mind the possibility of using some of these images from the video on the cover of a live album which was coming up shortly afterwards.

▷ I was interested in contrasting big close-ups of people (eyelashes, tip of nose, end of cuff, or shoelace) and very distant shots of the same people – figures in a very empty, featureless, almost linear landscape. A dry lake bed seemed ideal and we found one some three hours due east of Los Angeles. These figures represented songs ('Psychobabble') and graphic shapes (red balloons), and, of course, the odd joke (head in the clouds). Our photographer Paul Maxon took separate shots of the characters, or set ups, after we had filmed them for the video. The image opposite was intended to convey a sort of sci fi B feature kind of atmosphere, like a photographic still from *Outer Limits* or *Twilight Zone*. It had also to be cheap (for the video), hence a deluxe wardrobe of old macs and toyshop globes, but even so I think that Paul's pictures, and in particular his use of infra red black and white film, made the whole image work better than we had any right to expect.

▷ The other images are all dancing, all colour, bright and clear, taken for the most part in the heat of the day. This caused some consternation, and some bodily

above:

ALAN PARSONS "Live"
CD front [1995]

excretions, as you can readily appreciate, wearing dark suits and a 'cloud' in temperatures of 110 in the shade, which is where they were, of course, being directly in or under a cloud. These cloudheads (opposite) were graphically positioned, I trust you'll notice, above the horizon, in the sky area where they belong. ◁

The people with red industrial balloons (p168) were less inconvenienced, being in their braces and vests and no suffocating headgear. When let go, the balloons spluttered forward propelled by the air inside and bounced away from the figures, which looked more fab on film in reverse slow motion, bouncing back up to their mouths. The clamheads below are inexplicable and I suspect the responsibility of the artistically spontaneous, partially deranged, and very endearing Californian art department. ◁

I have to confess that I loved this location. It was vast, unencumbered, and great to look at in any direction, ie full 360 degrees, so it didn't matter much where you pointed the camera. It had superb and relatively constant lighting, decreasing only in the evening to produce warm orange tones and stupendous long Film Noir shadows. It was like a huge studio, a magic playground, and the crew and I could play freely with various toys (ideas, props and models) for a couple of days without interruption. And nobody there to tell us off.

(Weird) Animals

bite the hand that feeds

Chapter 6 (Weird) Animals

Ian Dury
Almighty
Thunder
Scottish Opera
Halloween
Quatermass
Ween

IAN DURY

Ian Dury is a legend in his own lunchtime. A philosopher from Essex, a dynamic, sounding off, very funny, offensive, narcissistic, unrepentant, opinionated, lovely chap. A wordsmith, a loudmouth and a teller of tales. A true survivor, not only of the transient world of popular music but also of polio, two virulent attacks of cancer, and the tragic death of his first wife. ◁

Feted and adored for 'Hit Me With Your Rhythm Stick', 'Sex And Drugs And Rock And Roll' and 'Reasons To Be Cheerful', Dury was 'forgotten' for years. As I write, his career is on an upward swing. 1998's *Mr Love Pants*, his first new record since 1981, was well received and his live performances with the infamous Blockheads are as funky as ever. The old bastard is back in vogue. ◁

Before *Mr Love Pants*, when things were quieter and Dury was in the recording doldrums, there was Repertoire Records from Hamburg. Their motto was 'Into the future with the past'. Resurrection by repackaging. *Reasons To Be Cheerful* was the album title of a collection of old Dury songs, and the cover was designed as a set of images to match. Pictures to make you smile, reasons to be cheerful. ◁

From the vast reservoir of bad puns and poor jokes embedded in the sludge of my brain came forth pictures to make you smile – a gift horse wrapped in ribbon, a jockey on a seahorse going nowhere fast, a fat unkissable frog with no chance of becoming a prince, and finally a deer with an eye, or an eye deer. A good idea. ◁

This awfully surreal image (or surreally awful image) appears on p3 and is produced as a single soft edged computer montage. The unkissable frog is in fact an unkissable toad which our lovely blonde model had

absolutely no intention of kissing, ever. The gift horse is being looked in the face by our very own Jon Crossland, normally sporting quite dapper attire but looking here a bit like a pervert in an overcoat. The seahorse being ridden by the overzealous jockey was awkward to shoot and necessitated a long trek to a seahorse aquarium in Exeter (never knew there was such a thing), and persuading my son to model for us, something he absolutely hates!

▷ Horses are an obscure theme for Dury and for me. Personally I'm scared of them. I think they are beautiful, powerful beasts, but they're too big and strong for my hairdresser mentality. I tried riding once in some woods in the south of France on holiday with my sister in law, and things were going great until my horse decided to

take a drink of water in a deep brook and headed down the steep and dangerous bank without warning (or permission) and took its drink but would not budge for half an hour or rejoin the others. I looked scared and foolish. In reality I was scared and foolish. In my imagination things are different and horses are more manageable, appearing on this page as yet another 'sea horse' – a horse made from the sea this time, slithers of water and shiny droplets forming its outline – or as formed by clothing blown in the air and entwined about itself in wavy shapes, suggesting an elegant and ethereal clothes horse – or as a black horse leaping over a sleeping figure at night, scaring her stupid, like a nightmare.

do you understand

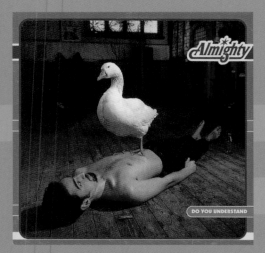

hard and quick. Could peck your eyes out. Which is, of course, why the man in the pictures here is pretty scared. Wouldn't you be? Never knowing at what moment the goose might strike. Goose gets heavy and pins human to the floor and demands its rights. "Don't fuck with me or I'll rearrange your eye balls. Do You Understand?" Goose power. I think this idea is just a silly thing. Absurd, because geese are absurd (no offence to geese lovers). Unlike the 'dog of despair' (p177), this image has no historical reference, no mythic context, no psychological implications. It's just a goose telling a geezer where it's at. That's all. The man is being goosed.

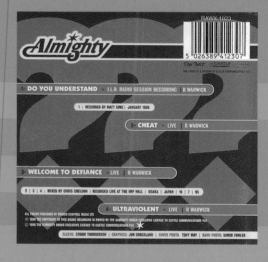

Don't work with animals or children' is an old maxim of the film business, for animals, and children to a lesser extent, do not read scripts. Animals will rarely do what you want, and normally do what you don't want. The answer is to get an expert. He won't necessarily do any better, but at least it's somebody else to blame. Our man Kevin Stinchcoombe is a totally excellent chap, forever optimistic despite continual animal perversity. Good humoured, honest West Country face, and hands like a meat loaf. Not the tidiest of chaps but fearless in the face of great (animal) odds. We used an owl once for a Floyd commercial for *Pulse*, which turned out fine eventually but only after a long and expensive day in the studio watching a variety of owls fly in the wrong direction, or at the wrong time, or at the wrong height, resisting enticement, persuasion or any technique that Kevin could devise. "You can't tell an owl what to do," he said wisely, owl like. Too damn right. You can't tell a goose either, but at least they don't fly so much. Kevin could pick it up and put it somewhere, and it might stay there, proud and disdainful, and if it didn't, Kevin would pick it up again and put it straight back. Show it who's boss, right? But geese bite

IAN DURY AND THE BLOCKHEADS "Mr Love Pants" CD front/back [1998]

dog's bollocks

After the relative commercial activity of *Reasons To Be Cheerful* (p170) Ian Dury embarked upon the release of his first new recording venture in 17 years. It was initially entitled 'Different Strokes', and we submitted various appropriate suggestions which were received in typical Dury fashion – jokes, quips, comments, anecdotes, questions and answers tumbling like a torrent, interwoven with word games, puns and assorted memories – only to find that he was unsure of the title. (That old chestnut again.) He was thinking of changing it to 'Mr Love Pants', what did we think? He grinned, knowing, I think, that this rendered our ideas inappropriate no matter what their intrinsic value. But it was a better title. It made me smile. I detected also that our ideas were not strong enough to persuade him otherwise, or stimulate a completely different title. ◁

Anyway I had an immediate idea which arrived on the mindscanner full and complete with all the intellectual trimmings and style elements (I even knew which dog). Ideas don't usually come so promptly – if only they did, I'd be a rich man and not sitting here talking to the likes of you. More often they are the result of endeavour and luck, and mind to mind interchange, but in this case there it was, resting warm and snug in my brain, bright and vivid, like the beach where it was set (see p174/5). "I love it," said Dury, panting breathlessly. ◁

We photographed the boxer dog several times in different locations and wearing several different shorts.

In the end they were specially made by the Andrea Galer fashion house (it was her dog after all). We then 'dropped' the preferred cut-out dog into a Caribbean background. Jon Crossland persuaded me, rightly, that it was the dog's expression which was crucial. It makes me smile to this day, for there he is grinning at us with quivering nostrils and lascivious eyes, dressed to kill in bright shiny green boxers, as only a boxer should, standing nonchalantly on a beach in Bermuda (as in Bermuda shorts), decorated with triangles (as in Bermuda triangle), and panting (with love) in true boxer style, with slobbery lips and lolling tongue, whilst planes and boats crash into the sea behind him. But none of this is very real, since the artwork is stuck

Mr LOVE PANTS

together in a slightly careless fashion, like a faked up tourist brochure.

▷ Jon Crossland took the theme of dogs and produced via the Mac computer using Freehand, Quark and old chewing gum the collage opposite for the CD booklet. Much of the original material was derived from old sources, ancient printed matter, then altered, distressed, scratched, reduced and changed beyond recognition – a sort of visual equivalent of 'sampling' – and amalgamated into a coherent vision, connected by dogs and dog themes. There were references to famous dogs like Lassie and Rin Tin Tin, to many odd looking breeds like poodles and whippets. To various expressions (dog's life, let sleeping dogs lie), the word 'dog' as adjective (dog fight, dog fish or dog rose), or to

different objects altogether (dog end, dog and bone, old sea dog) and so on and so forth. These witty allusions were principally intended to provide Jon with items to collage, secondly to provide design continuity, and thirdly to make you smile.

▷ I don't particularly like dogs but they figure quite prominently in my work. Don't get me wrong, I don't dislike them either. I might prefer cats in the flesh but not in design. Somehow dogs are more expressive. On this page, for example, is the shaggy greyhound travelling steadfastly at great speed, head to the wind, for Ian Dury's single 'Itinerant Child'. Then a sad-eyed Dalmatian from Catherine Wheel's *Like Cats And Dogs* (p30/31), a coiffured poodle from The Almighty's *Just Add Life* (p135), whose owner, I recall fondly, was coiffured in a similar fashion. And last, but by no means least, is the rough sketch for the Black Dog of Despair. It is said the Black Dog appears in our dreams, first at the gate, then on the path; then in later dreams at the front door, until finally, as death approaches, it is seen in the bedroom, and lastly sitting squarely on the chest, peering forward intently, suffocating the breath until one wakes up in a cold sweat. Be gone Black Dog.

THUNDER / A BETTER MAN

Since I think of myself primarily as a designer, or perhaps a conceiver – of ideas that is – I'm not as concerned with the technique, be it photographic or illustrative, as with the results. This is not a good thing. It stems from a mixture of indolence and apprehension. The former leads regrettably to impatience, wanting to secure the result quickly rather than taking care and pleasure in the arriving at it, whilst the apprehension leads, lamentably, to a reduced appreciation of the contribution of others. I am selfishly interested in how well the image conveys the idea, in how successfully the chosen medium expresses the intended feelings, rather than in its details or difficulties. But then, nobody's perfect.

▷ Actually this frog sitting on its rock is pretty nigh perfect, and is a splendid example of the opposite – it is an excellent photograph and very much appreciated. A brilliant capturing of the subject, though not by me. Most particularly for the pose – for once, it seems, an animal read the script, and adopted a great position totally in accord with directions. This frog is obviously from Rage or Storm (leading model agencies in London, I swear it). The catwalk, or frogwalk, would be no problem for this majestic amphibian. Such poise, such presence! Eat your heart out, Naomi. In addition the lighting, the setting and even the out of focus background, all work unselfishly to support the image.

▷ It's not often that a photograph so embodies the original concept as to take the breath away. I thought this photograph so humorous, so powerful, that I was tempted to use it as the front cover of this book, but then it might give the impression that this is a natural history book, or one of those detailed, illustrated books on English pond life. In real context, ie in the rock 'n' roll context, things were different and the frog worked in spectacular fashion, especially as a 60/40 street poster. We added an extra small inset picture of female lips to complement the flowers in the background, ie tulips (two lips) and to indicate the idea behind the unlikely image of a frog, and of course some lettering for the title. But that's all.

▷ This glistening fleshy beast will clearly turn into a handsome prince when kissed. He will be a 'better man' when released from the spell. Some sensitive lady, knowing intuitively how this water sodden creature could improve and become a better man (as they often do in real life), will give him that much needed release, that kiss of transformation. And if this kiss were enacted what a change there would be. What a celebration. What a sight. What a princely photograph! (Now, who was it who took this great shot?)

Tristan and Isolde

Talk about Judas; this Celtic story of *Tristan And Isolde* has more betrayal than the Last Supper, Shakespeare and Le Carré put together. Even the principal characters betray each other. So we're looking here for symbols of back stabbing, we're talking here of forked tongues, as in snakes, except we can't get snakes so easily in the UK and we had to settle instead for eels, glistening, wet and very snake like. A hundred of them slithering for real in a box in a studio. Maybe there's one in your bed, or even in your trousers? Or one in a condom, which we did many moons ago at Hipgnosis for a band called Birth Control. What kind of a name is that? Must've been a German band. But back to Wagner, who was definitely German. The really neat thing about this lot of entwined serpents is that they produced Celtic like shapes all on their own. Amazing. ◀

181

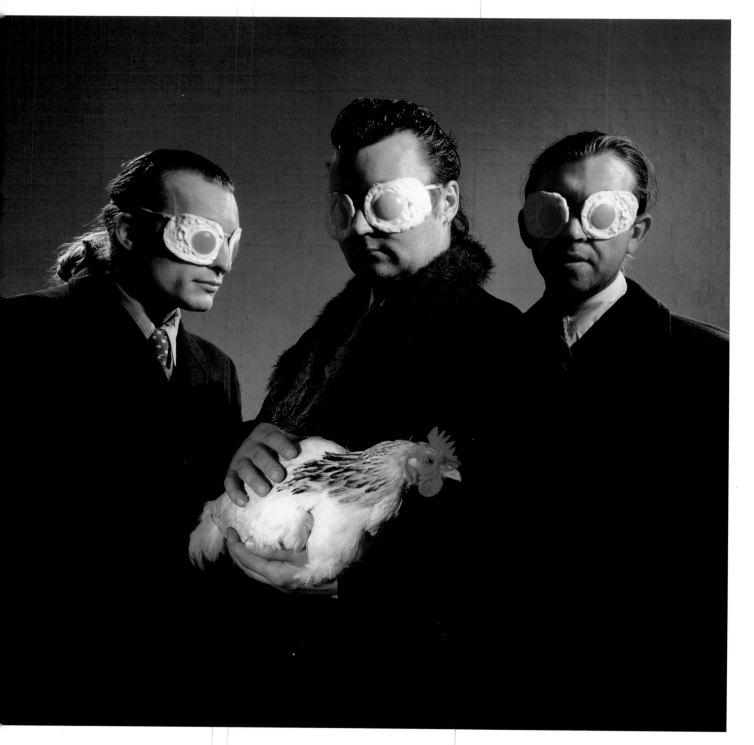

Which came first, the chicken or the egg? But why worry about egg on your face, unless you're Japanese? Or wetting the bed in the corridor of your mind? Or eating mackerel raw, if you're Japanese? Pterodactyls descend a modern skyscraper, the old and new, but not as new as the ancient scaly ichthyosaurus, which is, in fact, man of the distant future who wants to go swimming — no trunks needed, he just mutates into a swimming version. Evolution by design: and design is an evolutionary process, from the beginning. But which came first, the egg or the chicken?

HELLOWEEN "Pink Bubbles Go Ape" [circa 1990]   below: CD front / opposite: single bag

Hellow

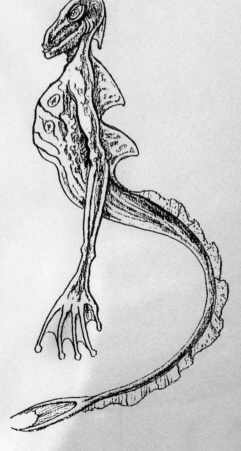

DOLLY (UNNATURAL EVOLUTION)

Ween is the collective name for two crazies from Philadelphia, two amiable tunesters who between them can play any instrument under the Pennsylvanian sun. They are called Gene Ween and Dean Ween respectively, can you believe that? Their attitude is anarchic, and their influences eclectic; thus all sorts of strange stuff, oddball mixtures of melody and rhythm, emanates from their music. There might be a Beatles like song followed by a heavy riff laden rocker, and then by an instrumental featuring a duet of dog barking and human burping. Next a wistful love song, then a sea shanty (parody), followed by a sad haunting piece and then a silly ditty or a Chinese spiritual (there's a thought). Ween's lyrics are tender, alliterative and disgusting. Eloquence and crudeness go hand in hand. Striking images are easily evoked amidst clever word play, sensitive observations, and cryptic descriptions. The whole Ween cosmos is underpinned by technical dexterity, catchy songs, and great ideas. ◁

So Gene and Dean, also known as Aaron and Mickey, ring me up, not from Pennsylvania, but Long Island, some studio by the sea, and tell me how their album is full of sea stuff, nautical references, images of sea monsters and sinking ships, mountainous waves, and strange creatures on the shore, or in the ocean, part real part imaginary. And they tell me, man, it's like your worst trip, a deeply bad acid trip, where you see yourself clinging to the wreckage of your boat, beset by tempestuous waves and icy winds, and then something slimy and horrible starts to entwine around your dangling legs and, then, man, y'know, it starts to consume you,

sucking life slowly out of your body, man, and then (warming to their task on the long distance phone) you wake up sweating in bed from this grotesque nightmare, this all time maritime bad acid experience, only to find that the wet slimy tentacled creature is really actually there in your bed (they pause overcome by their own descriptions). Holy shit.

▷ They subside. Something like that on the cover would be cool, they add, or anything else if you think of it.

▷ Well, we thought of some other things but Ween preferred the horrible creature now appearing on p187, more usually visible in the briny depths, or in the darker corners of the imagination. The dilemma here was how real or not to make it – too real then it might be familiar and not horrible enough, too unreal and it might be more magical than scary. We hoped that our nasty creature would have an edge to it since it was to be comprised of real (photographic) details that would be exaggerated or seen in unlikely conjunction. Finlay Cowan drew several versions modifying and amending as the creature evolved, indicating what real animals might supply what parts. His pencil design was used on the CD label. Sam Brooks and Rupert Truman began the long and tedious process of photographing numerous fish in numerous aquaria, including stone fish, flat fish, weird fish, crustacea, molluscs, cephalopods, jellyfish and nudibranches taken from a variety of angles. Then they embarked on the equally arduous process of picture selection and trial collage, adapting and amending as they went along. This is an essential procedure principally because reality and design rarely fit without a struggle – some fish parts proved better or worse than anticipated. About 30 or 40 different photographs, according to Finlay's original plan, were scanned into the computer, painstakingly cut out, assembled and then recoloured and resized where necessary.

▷ This is not only a long and expensive process but one requiring great skill. We could only manage this through the good offices of Jason Reddy, master retoucher, francophile and ex biker. Jason had learnt his craft on Paintbox and refined it on Mamba, but now uses Diacormid. Watching him work is impressive – he has a deft touch and great precision – since he requires more memory than the machine itself because of the need to

COPYRIGHT © ELEKTRA ENTERTAINMENT GROUP, A DIVISION OF WARNER COMMUNICATIONS INC. FOR THE UNITED STATES AND WEA INTERNATIONAL INC. FOR THE WORLD OUTSIDE THE U.S.A.

For Promotional use only. SALE OR OTHER TRANSFER IS PROHIBITED. MUST BE RETURNED ON DEMAND OF RECORDING COMPANY.

2-62013-P

ween
The Mollusk

ween 🦀 The Mollusk

perform tasks such that master scans, trial versions
and various layers can be summoned back and reinserted
where necessary. The machinery is extraordinary,
continually amazing me even though I've seen it function a
hundred times – it truly looks like magic, be it cloning, softening,
montaging, altering perspective, widening, stretching or
defocusing. However incredible the machinery it still doesn't
stop me remaining steadfastly a reactionary old toad. What I say
is...the machinery is only as good as the idea and the retoucher allow. The
computer is just a tool, albeit a fancy one, and not an artist (though I suppose that
one day it will be!). In many ways I don't like computers – they're kind of two faced
(two screened), seeming to offer multiple choice but in truth offering only a limited
choice (ie what's available on the software), far less than the choice available in
your own head. Not to mention that your head works in holistic changeable order,
whereas the computer, by and large, is linear and sequential. Better the computer
in your skull than the one on your desk. That's what I say.
◈ Peter took all the sundry elements and moulded them into a neat graphic
package using the Mac computer to combine elements and details into
graphicised fish and hybrid monsters of his own, as well as a
customised logo type for the band's name. Ween. Funny name.
What's it mean? One presumes that there is a
transatlantic verbal problem here, same word
different meanings, or same meaning different
words. Ween is from weenie, I guess, as in sausage (or
dick), from Wiener or Vienna sausage. A small dick as per
the Scottish wee or little one, the we'en of the family. Ween as
in wean, to remove from the breast. Gene and Dean Ween, the
terrible weenies, the troublesome teenies, inbetweenies, the not
so cleanies, but musical genies.

Why a duck?

Index

Storm Thorgerson

Born in Mutton Lane, Potters Bar, 15 miles north of London in 1944. Educated at Summerhill Free School, Brunswick Primary and Cambridge High School. BA Hons in English, Leicester University; and MA in Film & TV from the Royal College of Art. Self-taught photographer and graphic designer. Founded Hipgnosis with Po (Aubrey Powell) in 1968 (disbanded in 1983). Author of several books on album covers. Film director of numerous music videos, long forms, commercials and a few TV documentaries. Brought up one great son, Bill, 27. Now lives with Barbie, her two children and five cats in West Hampstead, London.

Peter Curzon

Ware, Hertfordshire, 1965. Educated in East Anglia and Herts. Ipswich Town FC. BTEC in Graphic Design at Colchester Institute, 1984. Punk. HND in Graphic Design at Barnet College, 1986. After graduating he worked with Keith Breeden and Martin Jenkins at DKB, designing covers for ABC, The Communards, The Gang Of Four and others. Mexico. Since 1992 he has been working for himself and on many varied projects with Storm, doing designs for airships, racing cars, CD ROMs, books and album covers. Eggnog. He and his partner Sally recently moved to East Finchley in North London.

Jon Crossland

Grew up in Walsall before attending St Martin's School of Art (BA Hons, Graphic Design) and quickly regressing. After graduating in 1987 he went to work as Neville Brody's assistant and attained a thorough grounding in the areas of stress and late night spray mount inhalation. Whilst with Nexus, a studio specialising in record sleeve design, he first encountered Storm. The rest is history (like the Franco-Prussian War or the Spanish Inquisition. Can I get my cheque now?). Faded glories include designing the 1989 Body Shop company report and dee-jaying for Clyde Stubblefield (the original James Brown funky drummer). Big shout out to Micci!

Tony May

Born 26.02.63 on a Devon farm overlooking the Taw Estuary. I should have been a farmer but fate pushed me towards biochemistry and, after much boredom, into photography and film. Met Storm by chance in 1986 on a shoot for Pink Floyd and it went on from there. We've done some of the best and most interesting shoots of my career and we're still friends. My philosophy has been not to question the brief too much but to enter into the spirit and push the boundaries of photography as far as possible. Recently I've been doing stills, promos and commercials. I consider myself lucky to have worked with Storm over many years.

Finlay Cowan

Born in 1966, Wallingford, Oxfordshire. Began work in 1987 as a metal sculptor and underground comic artist. In 1989 he began as a storyboard artist in advertising. He started working with Storm in 1993 designing album covers, stage films and promotional material for music industry clients. Between 1994 and 1996 he designed a number of covers for Bloomsbury Publishing including Will Self's Grey Area. In 1997 he joined Natalie Tate at Tate Management to research and develop ideas for TV and film. In his spare time he composes music and writes fiction. His specialist subject is RF Burton's translation of The Book Of A Thousand Nights And A Night. He is pictured with his son, Tyler.

Rupert Truman

Born 18 May 1960. Educated at Sir Walter St John's School, Battersea and at Kingston College of Further Education. Attended Kingston University (Bsc Hons in Geology). A short career in oil exploration ended when he became a freelance photographer in 1986. Rupert's work is very varied, much of it architectural, including work for The National Trust and books for Phaidon Press. Other recent clients include Management Today, Redwood Publishing and various interiors magazines. He and partner of 14 years, Penny, have two lovely, exhausting, expensive children, Kit and Joe.

Richard Manning

Born and lived in Chelmsford, Essex all my life (except two years in Kent when first married). School in Brentwood, Essex. Five year apprenticeship. Eighteen months as messenger. (For the purchase of one pair of Hush Puppies, managed to get a further two new pairs as they then carried a six month guarantee. Shortly after the third pair, the company withdrew the six month guarantee!) Met Storm in 1973 and began working for him. We never argued and always conversed pleasantly! Always worked in the West End – now almost entirely on Apple Mac. Married 1969, two children.

Sam Brooks

Born in Cornwall, 1971, Sam has lived in London since he was six. Always interested in things visual, he studied Art and Design at Central St Martin's in London and then Fine Art in Liverpool. Back in London after a year spent working in a film sound studio, he involved himself in making independent films as producer and art director. He first worked for Storm as an assistant and illustrator in 1996. After working nearly full time since, doing tasks as varied as restraining dogs to art directing photo shoots, he is now designing independently as 'Le Mutant'.

Jason Reddy

Born in Islington, North London in 1965. Educated in Buckinghamshire at Denbigh High School, then moved to Ireland. Two years later returned to London to continue his interest in Fine Art. After a mix of jobs in numerous studios, took the opportunity to learn photographic re-touching. In 1996, started his own re-touching studio in central London applying traditional photographic and modern computer techniques for ad agencies, designers, photographers and, of course, Storm. Now lives in Carshalton, Surrey with Rachel, their on-coming baby, and his two great daughters – Selen and Mailys.